BACH PERSPECTIVES

VOLUME 13

Bach Reworked

BACH PERSPECTIVES

VOLUME 13

Bach Reworked

Edited by
Laura Buch

UNIVERSITY OF
ILLINOIS PRESS
Urbana, Chicago, and Springfield

Library of Congress Cataloging-in-Publication Data
Names: Buch, Laura, editor.
Title: Bach reworked / edited by Laura Buch.
Description: Urbana : University of Illinois Press, 2020. | Series: Bach
perspectives; Volume 13. | Includes bibliographical references and index. |
Identifiers: LCCN 2020030549 (print) | LCCN 2020030550 (ebook) |
ISBN 9780252043635 (cloth) | ISBN 9780252052514 (ebook)
Subjects: LCSH: Bach, Johann Sebastian, 1685–1750—Criticism and
interpretation. | Bach, Johann Sebastian, 1685–1750—Influence. | Bach,
Johann Sebastian, 1685–1750—Influence. | Music—18th century—
History and criticism. | Parody in music. | Jazz—History and criticism.
Classification: LCC ML410.B13 B177 2020 (print) | LCC ML410.B13 (ebook)
| DDC 780.92—dc23
LC record available at https://lccn.loc.gov/2020030549
LC ebook record available at https://lccn.loc.gov/2020030550

CONTENTS

PREFACE

Much scholarly analysis and ingenuity has been devoted to the topic of parody and borrowing, with studies tracking the techniques across centuries and genres and with many of them focusing upon the works of Johann Sebastian Bach, well known for his abundant use of parody procedures. This topic inspired the April 2018 conference of the American Bach Society, held at Yale University, from which the present collection takes its title. All of the essays published here stem from earlier versions presented at this conference.

In reexploring such techniques, these essays unfold the subject in five different directions. What (and whom) do we mean by "Bach"? And what do we mean by "Reworked"? Both J. S. Bach and C. P. E. Bach are specifically examined; but the composer as symbol or cultural emblem—the lowercase "bach"—also rises for consideration. Similarly, Bach-reworking-others is counterbalanced by others-reworking-Bach, in performance and composition.

The first two essays remain in the eighteenth century. Markus Zepf reworks our understanding of Johann Caspar Ferdinand Fischer. While J. S. Bach's borrowings from Fischer are well known, Fischer's own background, training, and compositional techniques are less familiar. Zepf explores hearing Bach through Fischer but particularly extends the context for hearing Fischer himself, attending to his contrapuntal techniques in *Ariadne Musica* and to his own numerous borrowings from others.

Moira Leanne Hill examines the vast bounty of borrowings in Carl Philipp Emanuel Bach's Passions. Drawing upon his own works, as well as on those by many others (including J. S. Bach), C. P. E. Bach reworked both text and music. Hill considers his rationale for both, tracing examples through a representative sample of the twenty-one Passions that Bach wrote for Hamburg performances.

Erinn E. Knyt considers Ferruccio Busoni's adaptation of J. S. Bach's Goldberg Variations for the twentieth-century concert hall and examines Busoni's choices for restructuring, amplifying, and modifying the work. Her meticulous delineation of the work's performance history provides context for Busoni's reception during the century that also gave rise to the historically informed performance practice movement.

The remaining two essays investigate, respectively, Bach's appearances in the more recent realms of jazz and funk. Stephen A. Crist discusses Bach reworked by John Lewis and the Modern Jazz Quartet, with particular focus on their 1974 album *Blues on Bach*. Lewis's integration of Bach's contrapuntal works with the language of blues and his use of harpsichord—evoking, as Crist notes, "the imagined baroque"—reflect an important intersection of styles in a notable twentieth-century tribute to J. S. Bach.

Finally, Ellen Exner examines the influence of Bach upon keyboardist Bernie Worrell and the bands known collectively as Parliament-Funkadelic. Documenting Worrell's classical, conservatory training, Exner considers both the real and perceived traces of Bach in Worrell's keyboard improvisations and addresses the generic invocation of "bach" as cultural signifier.

I am grateful to the five authors in this collection for their essays and their kind collaboration, to the anonymous readers who reviewed the essays, and to Daniel R. Melamed for his invaluable expertise and advice. I thank the following for generously allowing us to reproduce images from their collections: the Staatsbibliothek zu Berlin—Preußischer Kulturbesitz, Musikabteilung mit Mendelssohn-Archiv; the Sing-Akademie zu Berlin; the Boston Symphony Orchestra; and Columbia Records/Rhino Entertainment Company.

Laura Buch, editor

ABBREVIATIONS

BG   *Bach-Gesellschaft Ausgabe*. Johann Sebastian Bach's complete works. Edited by the Bach-Gesellschaft. 47 vols. Leipzig: Breitkopf & Härtel, 1851–99, 1926.

BJ   *Bach-Jahrbuch*.

BR-CPEB   Wolfram Enßlin, Uwe Wolf, and Christine Blanken. *Carl Philipp Emanuel Bach. Thematisch-systematisches Verzeichnis der musikalischen Werke*. Pt. 2, *Vokalwerke*. Stuttgart: Carus, 2014.

BWV   [Bach-Werke-Verzeichnis.] *Thematisch-systematisches Verzeichnis der musikalischen Werke von Johann Sebastian Bach: Bach-Werke-Verzeichnis (BWV)*. Rev. ed. by Wolfgang Schmieder. Wiesbaden: Breitkopf & Härtel, 1990.

CPEB:CW   *Carl Philipp Emanuel Bach: The Complete Works*. Los Altos, Calif.: Packard Humanities Institute, 2005-.

D-B   Berlin, Staatsbibliothek zu Berlin—Preußischer Kulturbesitz, Musikabteilung mit Mendelssohn-Archiv.

D-LEb   Leipzig, Bach-Archiv.

FbWV   [Froberger-Werke-Verzeichnis.] Siegbert Rampe, ed. *Froberger. Neue Ausgabe sämtlicher Werke*. Vol. 7, *Ensemblewerke und Verzeichnis sämtlicher Werke (FbWV)*. Kassel: Bärenreiter, 2015.

FWV   [Fischer-Werke-Verzeichnis.] Klaus Häfner. "Johann Caspar Ferdinand Fischer und die Rastatter Hofkapelle. Ein Kapitel südwestdeutscher Musikgeschichte im Zeitalter des Barock." In *J. C. F. Fischer in seiner Zeit. Tagungsbericht Rastatt 1988*, edited by Ludwig Finscher, 137–79. Frankfurt am Main: Peter Lang, 1994.

GraunWV   [Graun-Werke-Verzeichnis.] Christoph Henzel. *Graun-Werkverzeichnis (GraunWV): Verzeichnis der Werke der Brüder Johann Gottlieb und Carl Heinrich Graun*. 2 vols. Beeskow: Ortus Musikverlag, 2006.

H   [Helm catalog number.] E. Eugene Helm. *Thematic Catalogue of the Works of Carl Philipp Emanuel Bach*. New Haven: Yale University Press, 1989.

HoWV   [Homilius-Werke-Verzeichnis.] Uwe Wolf. *Gottfried August Homilius. Thematisches Verzeichnis der musikalischen Werke (HoWV)*. Stuttgart: Carus, 2014.

HWV   [Händel-Werke-Verzeichnis] Bernd Baselt, ed. *Händel-Handbuch: Thematisch-systematisches Verzeichnis der musikalischen Werke von Georg Friedrich Händel*. 4 vols. Kassel: Bärenreiter, 1978–86.

L   [Lorenz catalog number.] Franz Lorenz. *Die Musikerfamilie Benda*. Vol. 3, "Themenkatalog der Kompositionen der Familienmitglieder mit durchnumeriertem Benda-Register." Unpublished typescript (1972) in D-B, Mus LS Tbe 3200.

NBA [Neue Bach-Ausgabe.] *Johann Sebastian Bach: Neue Ausgabe sämtlicher Werke*. Edited by Johann-Sebastian-Bach-Institut, Göttingen, and the Bach-Archiv, Leipzig. Kassel: Bärenreiter; Leipzig: Deutscher Verlag für Musik, 1954–2010.

NBR *The New Bach Reader: A Life of Johann Sebastian Bach in Letters and Documents*. Edited by Hans T. David and Arthur Mendel. Revised and enlarged by Christoph Wolff. New York: W. W. Norton and Co., 1998.

RISM *Répertoire International des Sources Musicales* (International Inventory of Musical Sources). Kassel: Bärenreiter; Munich: G. Henle, 1960-.

SA   Sing-Akademie zu Berlin (collection on deposit in D-B).

US-Bc Boston, New England Conservatory of Music, Harriet M. Spaulding Library.

US-NH New Haven, Yale University, the Irving S. Gilmore Music Library.

US-Wc Washington, D.C., Library of Congress, Music Division.

Wq   [Wotquenne catalog number] Alfred Wotquenne, *Thematisches Verzeichnis der Werke von Carl Philipp Emanuel Bach*. Leipzig: Breitkopf & Härtel, 1905.

Reworking Fischer

Some Observations about Johann Sebastian Bach and Johann Caspar Ferdinand Fischer

Markus Zepf

Little is known about the life of the keyboard virtuoso Johann Caspar Ferdinand Fischer. Most popular are his published works for stringed keyboard instruments: the suites *Les Pieces de Clavessin*, op. 2, published by the author in Schlackenwerth (Bohemia) in 1696, and two years later in a second edition titled *Musicalisches Blumen-Büschlein, Oder Neu eingerichtes Schlag-Wercklein*, which he issued in cooperation with Lorentz Kroniger and the heirs of Gottlieb Göbel in Augsburg. He also published an additional nine suites in Augsburg around 1738, titled *Musicalischer Parnassus*. Still more influential, however, was Fischer's collection for organ titled *Ariadne Musica*—a volume of twenty preludes and fugues with five ricercars based on hymns for the liturgical year, which he published in three editions in 1702, 1713, and 1715. Johann Sebastian Bach knew Fischer's *Ariadne Musica* and notably modeled a fugue subject in each book of *The Well-Tempered Clavier* on material from Fischer's collection. It is highly probable that Bach knew more of Fischer's printed music, at least. However, other musicians of the Bach family were also interested in Fischer's works. The so-called "Andreas-Bach-Buch," for example, compiled circa 1703–1713/14 by the Ohrdruf organist Johann Christoph Bach, contains a copy of Fischer's Praeludium VIII in G Major (FWV 16/1) together with the subsequent Chaconne (FWV 16/2),[1] both first published in opus 2. The Lowell Mason collection at Yale University preserves another manuscript with keyboard music from the Bach family, the so-called "Johann Günther Bach Book." In addition to works by Dieterich Buxtehude and Johann

---

1. Leipzig, Städtische Bibliotheken mit Musikbibliothek, Sammlung Becker, III.8.4, 214–16, accessed 29 January 2019, https://www.bach-digital.de/receive/BachDigitalSource_source_00003278. The Fischer-Werke-Verzeichnis (FWV) is given by Klaus Häfner, "Johann Caspar Ferdinand Fischer und die Rastatter Hofkapelle. Ein Kapitel südwestdeutscher Musikgeschichte im Zeitalter des Barock," in *Barock in Baden-Württemberg. Katalog zur Ausstellung im Badischen Landesmuseum Karlsruhe*, 2 (Karlsruhe: G. Braun Verlag, 1981), 213–32. Expanded in *J. C. F. Fischer in seiner Zeit. Tagungsbericht Rastatt 1988*, ed. Ludwig Finscher (Frankfurt am Main: Peter Lang, 1994), 137–79 (esp. 157–61).

Pachelbel, it also includes Bach's fifteen *Inventionen und Sinfonien* as well as a copy of Fischer's Preludium XIII in G Major (FWV 48) from *Ariadne Musica* (though without the fugue) and his ricercar on "Christ ist erstanden" (FWV 59), both without a named author.[2] Based on a copy from the collection of the singer and collector Franz Hauser, this ricercar was included in volume 40 of the *Bach-Gesellschaft Ausgabe* published in 1893, and later was listed as no. 746 in Wolfgang Schmieder's *Bach-Werke-Verzeichnis*, though Schmieder noted its origin.[3] In 1774, a quarter of a century after his father's death, Bach's second son, Carl Philipp Emanuel, reported to Johann Nikolaus Forkel on J. S. Bach's acquaintance with Fischer and other contemporaries: "Besides Froberger, Kerl and Pachelbel, he heard and studied the works of Frescobaldi, the Baden Capellmeister Fischer, Strunck, some old and good Frenchmen, Buxdehude, Reincken, Bruhns, and the Lüneburg organist Böhm."[4] These lines have proven to be reliable with the rediscovery of Fischer and his work in recent decades.

Who Is Fischer?

In 1719, Mauritius Vogt listed Fischer as collaborator of his *Conclave Thesauri Magnae Artis Musicae* and called him "nostri aevi Componista absolutissimus" (the most accomplished composer of our time)[5] but omitted biographical details, as did Johann Gottfried Walther in his *Musicalisches Lexicon* in 1732.[6] Eight decades later, Ernst Ludwig Gerber commented that Fischer was an accomplished keyboard virtuoso who was renowned for the execution of ornaments as well as for his good taste in performing keyboard music in the German-speaking countries ("Fischer . . . gehörte unter die stärksten Klavierspieler seiner Zeit, und hat den Ruhm, die Bezeichnung der Manieren, so wie den guten Vortrag überhaupt auf diesem Instrumente in Deutschland

2. US-NH, Lowell Mason collection, LM 4983, p. 3 (FWV 48) and p. 56 (FWV 59), accessed 29 January 2019, https://www.bach-digital.de/receive/BachDigitalSource_source_00004299. See Yoshitake Kobayashi, "Der Gehrener Kantor Johann Christoph Bach (1673–1727) und seine Sammelbände mit Musik für Tasteninstrumente," in *Bachiana et alia Musicologica. Festschrift Alfred Dürr zum 65. Geburtstag am 3. März 1983*, ed. Wolfgang Rehm (Kassel: Bärenreiter, 1983), 168–77.

3. See Ernst Naumann, ed., BG 40, l; and see "BWV 746," in BWV 1950, 461.

4. NBR, 398–400, no. 395 (quote on 398). C. P. E. Bach's list of composers refers to Johann Jacob Froberger, Johann Caspar Kerll, Johann Pachelbel, Girolamo Frescobaldi, Johann Caspar Ferdinand Fischer, Delphin Strungk, Dieterich Buxtehude, Johann Adam Reincken, Nicolaus Bruhns, and Georg Böhm.

5. Mauritius Vogt, *Conclave Thesauri Magnae Artis Musicae* (Prague: Magnum Collegium Carolinum, 1719), fol. 1v.

6. Johann Gottfried Walther, *Musicalisches Lexicon oder Musicalische Bibliothec* (Leipzig: Deer, 1732), 246.

verbreitet und bekannt gemacht zu haben").[7] Only a few such ornaments are given by Fischer in a figure following his introduction to *Les Pieces de Clavessin* and the subsequent *Musicalisches Blumen-Büschlein* in 1698, but there is no hint by contemporaries regarding Fischer's execution of them.[8] Because Fischer died on August 27, 1746, in Rastatt[9] and Ernst Ludwig Gerber was born four weeks later on September 29, 1746, the latter could not have had recourse to experiences of his own in this regard; it thus seems probable that Gerber instead relied on his father's statements for his description of Fischer's playing. Heinrich Nikolaus Gerber had studied keyboard instruments and basso continuo with Johann Sebastian Bach in Leipzig from 1724 until at least 1727 and had stayed in touch with him during the following years.[10]

Fischer's education as well as his musical training are unknown. In the first half of the twentieth century, the Prague musicologist and lawyer Emilián Trolda collected numerous copies of Czech baroque music of the seventeenth and eighteenth centuries and in 1949 bequeathed his valuable collection to the music division of the National Museum in Prague.[11] His collection includes seven copies of works by Fischer, which Trolda found in such Bohemian archives as those of "the Knights of the Cross with the Red Star" in Prague. In the 1970s, additional works by Fischer were uncovered by Tomislav Volek in Bohemian musical inventories. In keeping with the dictum "bohe-

7. Othmar Wessely, ed., *Ernst Ludwig Gerber: Neues historisch-biographisches Lexikon der Tonkünstler* (Graz: Akademische Druck- und Verlagsanstalt, 1966), vol. 1, cols. 134–35 (quote on col. 134).

8. Bach himself, however, provided a more detailed table of ornaments on fol. 3v in his *Clavier-Büchlein vor Wilhelm Friedemann Bach*; see NBA V/5 (ed. Wolfgang Plath; 1962), 3. His table is indeed a shorter compilation from the editions of Jean-Henri d'Anglebert and Nicolas de Grigny; see David Schulenberg, *The Keyboard Music of J. S. Bach*, 2nd ed. (New York: Routledge, 2006), 165.

9. Ernst von Werra, ed., introduction to *J. C. F. Fischer. Sämtliche Werke für Klavier und Orgel* (Leipzig: Breitkopf & Härtel, 1901; reprint, *Sämtliche Werke für Tasteninstrument [Cembalo, Orgel, Klavier]*, Wiesbaden: Breitkopf & Härtel, 1983), xiv, cites 27 March 1746 as Fischer's date of death. This stems from a misreading by the Catholic parish office of St. Alexander in Rastatt, which had provided the dates to von Werra. The short record for 27 August 1746 reads: "Casparus Fischer, rite provisus" (Caspar Fischer, provided with the last sacraments); see parish office, St. Alexander in Rastatt, "Totenbuch 1724–1751," p. 42. Despite its brevity, this record undoubtedly concerns the *Kapellmeister* Johann Caspar Ferdinand Fischer, because at the beginning of January 1747 Margrave Ludwig Georg appointed Franz Ignaz Zwiebelhofer to be Fischer's successor as *Kapellmeister*. See Rüdiger Thomsen-Fürst, *Studien zur Musikgeschichte Rastatts im 18. Jahrhundert*, Stadt Rastatt. Stadtgeschichtliche Reihe, vol. 2 (Frankfurt am Main: Peter Lang, 1996), 98–110 (esp. 99–100).

10. Andreas Glöckner, "Heinrich Nikolaus Gerber," in *The New Grove Dictionary of Music and Musicians*, 2nd ed. (London: Macmillan, 2001), 9:686.

11. John Tyrell, "Trolda, Emilián," in *New Grove Dictionary*, 25:756–57.

mica non leguntur," these discoveries have long remained unknown outside of the former Czechoslovakia. For that reason, the scholar Rudolf Walter published titles from
Trolda's collection and some of Volek's discoveries in the German journal *Archiv für
Musikwissenschaft* in 1975.[12] In Schlan (thirty kilometers northwest of Prague) around
1970, for example, Volek discovered that the "Order of Poor Clerics Regular of the
Mother of God of the Pious Schools" (Piarists) had purchased the hymn *Deus tuorum
militium*, à 7 (SSATB, two violins), in 1680. In the Schlan inventory, it is listed with
the note "author: Fischer Rhetore Slakowerdensi."[13] According to Volek and Walter,
there is little doubt that this meant Johann Caspar Ferdinand Fischer. The Latin term
"Slakowerdensi" refers to Schlackenwerth (now Ostrov nad Ohři), located between
the famous spa town of Carlsbad (Karlovy Vary) and Sankt Joachimsthal (Jáchymov)
in northwestern Bohemia. In 1623, Duke Julius Heinrich of Sachsen-Lauenburg, who
resided in Ratzeburg near Lubeck in Northern Germany, purchased the village and
manor of Schlackenwerth from his employer, the emperor Ferdinand I; in the following years, Julius Heinrich resided in numerous nearby villages and spent most of
his time in his new favorite locale. In the year after his death in 1665, his third wife,
Anna Magdalena Popelia (née Lobkowitz), founded a house of the Piarist order, with
Latin school and monastery, north of the castle grounds. Latin and especially music
education were parts of the curriculum. The record of the Schlan inventory indicates
that Fischer completed the highest level class in Schlackenwerth and received parts
of his musical training there.

It is hardly surprising that Duke Julius Franz, who reigned from 1666, entrusted the
Piarists with the education of his daughters, Anna Maria Franziska and the younger
Franziska Sibylla Augusta.[14] According to Fischer's dedication in the second edition
of opus 2, the marchioness Sibylla Augusta played the clavichord well—a skill she
could have acquired with the Piarists. Nevertheless, Fischer's education and musical
training following this era are still unknown. In view of the counterpoint techniques
examined in manuscripts of Fischer's Mass settings, Rudolf Walter conjectured (though
unconvincingly) that Fischer had studied with Christoph Bernhard in Dresden, around

12. Rudolf Walter, "Zu J. C. F. Fischers geistlicher Vokalmusik. Neue Funde," *Archiv für Musikwissenschaft* 32 (1975): 39–71.

13. Communications from Tomislav Volek to Rudolf Walter. See Walter, "Fischers geistlicher Vokalmusik," 49n51.

14. All dates concerning local history are drawn from Markus Zepf, "Markgräfin Sibylla Augusta als
Regentin," in *Extra Schön. Markgräfin Sibylla Augusta und ihre Residenz. Eine Ausstellung anläßlich des 275.
Todestages der Markgräfin Sibylla Augusta von Baden-Baden* (Petersberg: Michael Imhoff, 2008), 27–41.
Also see Rudolf Walter, *Johann Caspar Ferdinand Fischer. Hofkapellmeister der Markgrafen von Baden*,
Quellen und Studien zur Musikgeschichte von der Antike bis in die Gegenwart, vol. 18 (Frankfurt
am Main: Peter Lang, 1990), 64–88.

150 kilometers from Schlackenwerth.[15] One need not look far, however, for another possibility: that Fischer studied with his predecessor, Augustin Pfleger. According to a note by Franz Ludwig, Duke Julius Franz appointed Pfleger as *Kapellmeister* in 1680.[16] In Schlackenwerth on July 22, 1686, Pfleger married Maria Margaretha Frölligin (Fröhlich), the daughter of the duke's bookkeeper, Anton Cornelius Fröllig.[17]

While Ernst von Werra published his painstakingly collected biographical dates in his reliable editions of Fischer's keyboard works in 1901, Fischer's date and place of birth remained unknown. Werra's edition, however, gave Fischer scholars a fresh impetus, for example inspiring a comprehensive and stimulating paper by Richard Hohenemser the following year.[18] In 1906, Johann Haudeck suggested that Fischer was born in the village of Schönfeld, near the Tepl abbey, around thirty kilometers south of Carlsbad. Haudeck attributed his hypothesis to a hint given in Jan Bohumír Dlabacz's three-volume *Allgemeines historisches Künstler-Lexicon für Böhmen* (Prague, 1815)—however, this work contains no clue about Johann Caspar Ferdinand Fischer. In the Schönfeld baptismal registers, Haudeck discovered only a "Johann Fischer," baptized as the son of a miner and a flute player in 1635, but had ruled him out, since Fischer's opus 1 (the orchestral suites, *Le Journal du Printems* [*sic*]) was published in 1695, and his *Musicalischer Parnassus* circa 1738. He had overlooked a seemingly relevant record, which was eventually presented by Tomislav Volek at the symposium on Fischer held in October 1988 in Rastatt (the town where Fischer had lived from at least 1715 until his death in 1746).[19] In his paper, Volek surprised the scholarly com-

---

15. Walter, *Johann Caspar Ferdinand Fischer*, 48–49.

16. The certificate of appointment was first mentioned in Franz Ludwig, "Neue Forschungen über den Markgräflich-Badischen Hofkapellmeister Johann Kaspar Ferdinand Fischer," *Mitteilungen des Vereins für die Geschichte der Deutschen in Böhmen* 49 (1911): 71–78 (quote on 71n2). This certificate was unknown to Annemarie Nausch, *Augustin Pfleger-Leben und Werke. Ein Beitrag zur Entwicklungsgeschichte der Kantate im 17. Jahrhundert* (Kassel: Bärenreiter, 1954).

17. State Archive Pilzen, "Kirchenbuch Schlackenwerth," vol. 5, Abt. Copulationen, fol. 48r, accessed 29 January 2019, http://www.portafontium.eu/iipimage/30066695/ostrov-05_0183-0?x=-27&y=-51&w=1343&h=540. According to these parish church records, Pfleger and his wife served six times as godparents or witnesses, with the last instance on 22 July 1688; see ibid., fol. 325v, baptismal record of Maria Anna Elisabeth Friedrich, daughter of the princely trumpeter Matthes [= Matthias] Friedrich and his wife, Waberl. One of six witnesses was Maria Margaretha Pfleger.

18. Richard Hohenemser, "J. K. F. Fischer als Klavier- und Orgelkomponist," *Monatshefte für Musik-Geschichte* 34 (1902): 154–63, 167–76, and 183–86. Hohenemser classifies the suites for harpsichord, the organ versets, *Blumen Strauss* (printed in Augsburg at an unknown time, perhaps posthumously, acccording to the preface), and last but not least *Ariadne Musica* in the context of south German music but reasonably compares some details with Bach and George Frideric Handel.

19. The proceedings of the symposium were published in Finscher, *J. C. F. Fischer in seiner Zeit*.

munity with his discovery that Fischer was baptized as a tailor's son on September 7, 1656, in Schönfeld. While Volek unfortunately did not publish the paper, Rudolf Walter followed these traces behind the Iron Curtain and obtained access to the Schönfeld records.[20] Since then, the registers have become available online and can be accessed by the scholarly community. The baptismal record reads: "Anno 1656 . . . Die 7. Septembr: Baptizatus est infans no[min]e Johannes parens Wolff Fischer sartor hic | patrini Johannes Mesner, alter Kilian Rath patrina Maria Grimmischin" (In the year 1656 . . . September, 7: A child named Johannes was baptized. Father is Wolff Fischer, tailor of our city, godfather is Johannes Mesner, the other one Kilian Rath and Maria Grimmischin the godmother).[21] The parents, Wolfgang Fischer (baptized there on September 11, 1628) and Anna, née Vogel (baptized on April 28, 1626), were married on November 26, 1651, in Schönfeld.[22]

Both Rudolf Walter and Tomislav Volek trusted Haudeck's assumption with certainty, but there remain some doubts. Schönfeld, in Bohemia, is located about thirty kilometers south of Schlackenwerth; and the record for the Schlan hymn noted Fischer as a pupil in the highest level class at the Piarist Latin school in Schlackenwerth. Is it possible for a tailor's son to attend a school more than thirty kilometers distant, and furthermore in a duke's residence? Was the father required to pay for an accommodation in Schlackenwerth, or did his son get a grant? These questions cast doubt upon whether the Schönfeld baptismal record is indeed the one for Johann Caspar Ferdinand Fischer, especially as the indication "Rhetore Slakowerdensi" also can be read as an indication of his birth in Schlackenwerth. This objection becomes still more solid when considering that the child—honoring his first godfather—was only baptized "Johann"; the name of the second godfather, Kilian, is not included (contrary to convention) as part of his name. In contradiction to this, in church records as well as other documents and on most title pages, the eventual *Kapellmeister* is identified as "Johann Caspar Fischer" or (on title pages of some prints) as "Johann Caspar Ferdinand

20. It is currently unknown if Walter got firsthand access or obtained the information through an archive employee. See Walter, *Johann Caspar Ferdinand Fischer*, 16–17; also see Rudolf Walter, "Fischer, Johann Caspar Ferdinand," in *Lexikon zur deutschen Musikkultur Böhmen, Mähren, Sudetenschlesien* (München: Langen Müller, 2000), vol. 1, cols. 630–38; Rudolf Walter, "Fischer, Johann Caspar Ferdinand," in *Die Musik in Geschichte und Gegenwart*, 2nd ed., Personenteil, vol. 6 (Kassel: Bärenreiter, Metzler, 2001), cols. 1250–56; and Rudolf Walter, "Fischer, Johann Caspar Ferdinand," in *New Grove Dictionary*, 8:893–96.

21. State Archive Pilzen, Schönfeld parish records (Sbírka matrik západních Čech), no. 1014, vol. 2, "Taufregister," 1625–1660, fol. 77v., accessed 29 January 2019, http://www.portafontium.eu/register/soap-pn/krasno-02.

22. Ibid., "Taufregister," 12v: Wolfgang Fischer; "Taufregister," 4r: Anna Vogel; "Copulationsregister," fol. 101v.

Fischer," but never merely as "Johann Fischer." The question must be asked: why and on which occasion should he have added the second name, "Caspar"?

I discussed this problem extensively, in June and July 2014, with Mrs. Gabriele Wiechert (Sulzbach/Taunus), who is a descendant of Johann Caspar Ferdinand Fischer and strongly interested in genealogy. She pointed me to pertinent online records and to the likelihood, according to her, that Fischer was a native of Schlackenwerth, not Schönfeld. The baptismal register in Schlackenwerth records on June 18, 1662: "Infans: Johann Caspar. Parentes: Hanns Fischer Die Mutter Catharina." It lists the godfather, Johann Stichenwirt, and the witnesses Caspar Lihl, a white tanner, and Anna Krimig.[23] So, these baptismal records initially gave the impression that Wiechert was correct and that the Fischers were an integral part of the local craftsmen society; but my objection was that "Fischer," nowadays, is quite a common surname. Consequently, for this essay I examined the baptismal register between 1656 (following Volek's discovery) and 1664 (the end of the current register) and made the startling discovery that only four children surnamed "Fischer" had been baptized at Schlackenwerth's parish church during this period. Looking further into the first names "Johann Caspar," I learned that only seven children in as many families were named in this way in Schlackenwerth during this period. Most importantly: no other "Johann Fischer" or "Johann Caspar Fischer" was baptized in Schlackenwerth in the period mentioned. In other words, the surname "Fischer" was not all too frequent in Schlackenwerth, and the possibility of Wiechert having discovered the birth date and place of an eminent musician is highly probable and nearly certain. Nevertheless, one question remains unanswered: on which occasion did he add "Ferdinand"? Since this name is known only from title pages, it could have been used to distinguish his self-published works from those by any other author potentially named "Johann Fischer."

According to Carl Philipp Emanuel Bach, as quoted above, J. S. Bach was familiar with works by Fischer. Did they know each other in person? While Carl Philipp Emanuel Bach remains silent on this, the following circumstances could have provided an opportunity for the two to meet. The distance between Rastatt and Cöthen is about 580 kilometers, but between Schlackenwerth and Carlsbad only 15 kilometers. Pater Martinus a Sancto Brunone (Johann Georg Jacob Schubart, from Vienna)[24] was the

23. State Archive Pilzen, Schlackenwerth parish records (Sbírka matrik západních Čech), no. 1014, vol. 4, "Taufregister," 1627–1664, 318, accessed 29 January 2019, http://www.portafontium.eu/iipimage/30066694/ostrov-04_0166-n. It should be pointed out that this record is missing in the index of the Schlackenwerth church records, made in 1834 by the priest Anton Melzer and his vicar Franz Hohenrichter; see ibid., vol. 74, accessed 29 January 2019, http://www.portafontium.eu/iipimage/30066764/ostrov-74_0010-x?x=-103&y=347&w=1137&h=457.

24. Karl A. F. Fischer, *Verzeichnis der Piaristen der deutschen und böhmischen Ordensprovinz* (Munich: R. Oldenbourg, 1985), 133.

first prior of the Piarists' house in Rastatt, founded by Marchioness Sibylla Augusta in June 1715. His handwritten chronicle begins with the founding in 1715 and ends in December 1719. In it, he noted that Fischer twice spent three months in Schlacken-werth—his first stay beginning in May 1716 and his second in June 1717—to resolve inheritance cases. (Unfortunately, he provided no further details, mentioning only that, during Fischer's absence, Pater Oswaldus à Sancta Caecilia [Ferdinand Richter, from Carlsbad] held the music lessons and conducted the court musicians.)[25] It is easily conceivable that Fischer was indeed in Schlackenwerth while Bach resided there in the entourage of Duke Leopold of Anhalt-Cöthen in the summer of 1720; however, this remains unknown.

Ariadne Musica: Fischer's Last and
Most Distinguished Work

One may turn with more certainty to Fischer's collection of preludes and fugues, *Ariadne Musica*, op. 4. While Johann Sebastian Bach's two books of *The Well-Tempered Clavier* are well-known and have been subjects of critical analysis, Fischer's collection is mostly mentioned on the sidelines as their more or less important predecessor. Organists, especially, often greet *Ariadne Musica* with a smile, due to the brevity of its preludes and fugues. But what indeed is this work about?

One may begin with the history of the print. Consisting of twenty preludes and fugues, with an appendix of five ricercars on liturgical hymns, this collection was self-published by Fischer in 1702. Although mentioned by Johann Gottfried Walther in 1732, no extant copy of this original print is known. But a composite manuscript in the music library of the Minorites order in Vienna includes the *Musicalisches Blumen-Büschlein*, op. 2, followed by parts of *Ariadne Musica*; the latter is described as "Incipiunt Praeludia, et Fugae ejusdem Authoris [= Fischer] ex o[mn]ibus clavibus. Opus Quartum Slacoverdae. Ariadne musica. Neo-Organoedum. Per Viginti Praeludia totidemq[ue]. Fugas" (The beginning of Preludes and Fugues, in all keys, by the same author. Opus four, Schlackenwerth. Ariadne musica. For the new organist [or beginner]. In twenty preludes and as many fugues). This anonymous copy is dated November 12, 1704,[26] and therefore serves as an important corroboration of Walther's accuracy. Additionally, it indicates that Fischer had once again self-published his work and had included—un-like in his two later editions of the collection—"Opus 4" on its title page.

---

25. Ibid., 144; see "Memorabilia Statum Initij & Progressus Collogij & Gymnasij . . . Rastadij," manu-script in library of Ludwig-Wilhelm-Gymnasium Rastatt (lacks shelf mark), 40–41 (May 1716) and 84 (June 1717).

26. See Friedrich Wilhelm Riedel, *Das Musikarchiv im Minoritenkonvent zu Wien (Katalog des älteren Bestandes vor 1784)*, Catalogus musicus, vol. 1 (Kassel: Bärenreiter, 1963), no. 702.

In 1713, Fischer published a second edition of *Ariadne Musica* in Vienna, where today its one and only copy is preserved in the archive of the Minorites.[27] The score is engraved but the title page is typeset and now identifies the author as "Serenissimi Principis Ludovici Marchionis Badensis olim Capellae Magistri" (formerly *Kapellmeister* of the Most Serene Margrave Ludwig Wilhelm of Baden). Margrave Ludwig Wilhelm had died on January 4, 1707, in his new residence in Rastatt, and Fischer's career subsequently remains undocumented until October 1715. The publisher of the 1713 edition was Adam Damer at Zwettler Hof in Vienna—the location of the Cistercian abbey Zwettl (Lower Austria). This print is dedicated to Peter Ferdinand Rorer, doctor of law, canon at St. Stephen's Cathedral in Vienna, and counselor of the emperor's consistory,[28] with the dedication signed by Damer, not by Fischer.[29]

According to Friedrich W. Riedel, the same plates were reused for the 1715 edition of the collection by Joseph Friedrich Leopold in Augsburg. The new title page is engraved, as is Fischer's dedication to Raimund Wilfert II (1688–1724), abbot of the Premonstratensian abbey in Tepl. RISM lists nine extant copies of the 1715 edition.[30] Ernst von Werra lists an additional copy at the Berlin Staatsbibliothek, with a title page in the hand of Johann Nicolaus Forkel that replicates that of the 1715 print.[31] The other copy in Berlin (shelf mark: Am.B. 376) formerly belonged to the collection of the Joachimsthalsche Gymnasium and was once part of the library of Prussian princess Anna Amalia; it includes the signature "[Johann Philipp] Kirnberger" on its title page. This copy contains Fischer's dedication—with its elaborate Latin devotional praise of the abbot—which is not preserved in all copies but which Ernst von Werra reprinted in his edition (see Figures 1.1 and 1.2).[32]

27. See RISM A/I, F 982.

28. Riedel, *Das Musikarchiv*, no. 689.

29. Friedrich Wilhelm Riedel, "Johann Caspar Ferdinand Fischers Kompositionen für Tasteninstrumente in ihrer Bedeutung für die Stilentwicklung am Wiener Hof," in Finscher, *J. C. F. Fischer in seiner Zeit*, 45–54 (quote on 47).

30. RISM A/I, F 983; these nine copies are preserved in Brussels, Einsiedeln, Müstair, Berlin, Karlsruhe, Regensburg, Dresden, Paris, and Washington, D.C. The copy at US-Wc has been published in facsimile; see Performer's Facsimiles, 197 (New York: Broude Brothers, 1997).

31. This print (shelf mark: Mus. O. 9140 Rara) is not listed in RISM, but it is still available at D-B, according to Dr. Roland Schmidt-Hensel (D-B, Music Division), kind communication to author, 28 January 2019.

32. For further details, see von Werra, *Sämtliche Werke für Klavier und Orgel*, x (available online at imslp.net). All examples from Fischer's printed works in the present essay are also based on von Werra's edition.

Ioannis Caspari Ferdinandi Fischer

Serenissimi Principis Ludovici Marchionis Badensis

olim Capellae Magistri

ARIADNE MUSICA

Neo-Organoedum

Per Viginti Praeludia, totidem Fugas atque Quinque Ricer-

caras Super totidem Sacrorum anni Temporum Ecclesiasticas

Cantilenas è difficultatum labyrintho educens,

Opus praestantissimum ultimumque

Magistris aeque ac Discipulis virtute et utilitate maxime commendandum

August. Vindelicorum, prostat apud Josephum Frid. Leopoldum.

Anno 1715.

Figure 1.1. Title page of J. C. F. Fischer, *Ariadne Musica*, Augsburg, 1715.
Ernst von Werra, ed., *Sämtliche Werke für Klavier und Orgel*, 75.

Reverendissime Perillustris ac Amplissime Domine!

Ariadnen Sisto, non quidem commentitiam illam, Poetarumque versibus decantatam, sed aliam, talemque, ut, quod in illa videbatur verisimile, in hac ipsissima veritas appareret. Si enim illa Theseum Herculeae fortitudinis aemulum Cretensis Labyrinthi periculis, et periculosis viarum ambagibus per alligatum in limine filum ad nominis immortalitatem in occiso Minotauro comparandam induxit, et securissime eduxit; Haec Neo-Organoedum, vel in ipso artis limine difficultatum plurimarum Labyrintho deviantem, et errorum gravissimorum pericula formidantem, Praeludiorum suorum, Fugarumque filo suavissime diriget, ipsissimasque difficultatum vias percurrere, errorum Minotaurum jugulare docebit, et ad gloriam obtinendam securissime deducet. Non tamen ab Organoedis, ut illa a Theseo derelicta, derelinqui, sed foveri desiderans, amplexui *Reverendissimae, Perillustris ac Amplissimae Dominationis Vestrae*, qua potest verborum et affectuum humanitate, se insinuat; non eo tantum nomine, quod sciat, hic omnium ingeniorum conatus provocari, et admitti, sed memor, quantis gratiarum favoribus, licet indignissima, fuerit delibuta, dum vel in sui parte coram *Reverendissima Perill. Ac Ampl. Dom. Vestra* Compareret; audacior facta, se totam Ejusdem devotissimo obsequio repraesentatura, fores pulsat gratiarum, admitti, et una secum *Rever. Perill. Ac Ampl. Dom. Totique Celeberrimae Canoniae Teplensi* tot populorum vota adferri desiderans, quot claves, tot animorum affectus, quot notas, tot ad utriusque hominis exigentiam prosperitates, quot pausas et suspiria, tot felicissimos annorum ambitus, quot apices continet. Haec dum illa animitus apprecatur, Ego me subscribo et maneo

Reverendissimae Perillustris ac Amplissimae Dominationis Vestrae

Servus humillimus

J. C. F. Fischer.

Figure 1.2. Dedication of J. C. F. Fischer, *Ariadne Musica*, Augsburg, 1715.
Ernst von Werra, ed., *Sämtliche Werke für Klavier und Orgel*, 76.

This dedication is instructive about the collection's structure and offers an unusual hint regarding the ancient myth of Theseus, who fought against the cruel Minotaur, caught in a labyrinth on Crete. To help him find his way back through the labyrinth's confusing turns, the king's daughter Ariadne gave Theseus a thread before he started on his dangerous excursion. Fischer alludes to this myth in his dedication, especially to the brave Theseus and his victorious return. In the same way, the tutor Fischer wishes to lead the "Neo-Organoedus" through the dangers of liturgical organ playing, as well as those of modulations to the more distant keys that became possible in the German-speaking countries in the last third of the seventeenth century.[33] These pieces therefore presume a fully chromatic keyboard without a split octave and especially a well-tempered tuning in order to make a tonic possible on every key. In his repeatedly published lexicon article about Fischer, Rudolf Walter suggested,

> Fischer's bold venture [of *Ariadne musica*] was probably the result of cooperation with an organ builder who had a liking for experiments. With the consent of Abbot Raimund Wilfert of Tepl, to whom *Ariadne musica* is dedicated, Fischer and Abraham Stark (1659–1709), an organ builder from Elbogen, tuned the choir organ of Tepl monastery to something approaching equal temperament in 1700. Their success was followed by the composition and printing of *Ariadne musica*, an experiment which Fischer repeated, although with fewer keys, in the litanies printed in 1711. He later added a conservative appendix to *Ariadne*: five ricercares on Catholic hymns, preludes to the main feasts of the church year.[34]

To play *Ariadne Musica*, a well-tuned temperament is indispensable, whether on organ or on stringed keyboard instruments. But, as far as I can see, there is no evidence that Stark tuned to equal temperament following Fischer's instructions or after a meeting in person. Documented, however, are the stop lists of Stark's two organs in the Tepl abbey church. The larger instrument was begun by Peter Dottenius from Prague in 1694 and was completed after his death by Abraham Stark in October 1696. Following this, Raimund Wilfert ordered a new choir organ with ten stops, one keyboard, and pedal, which Stark built in 1700.[35]

33. See, for example, Andreas Werckmeister, *Musicalische Temperatur* (Frankfurt/Oder: Theodor Philipp Calvisius, 1691), accessed 29 January 2019, http://digital.slub-dresden.de/werkansicht/dlf/11688/1/; also see Werckmeister, *Erweiterte und verbesserte Orgel-Probe* (Quedlinburg: Theodor Philipp Calvisius, 1698), 79, accessed 29 January 2019, http://digital.slub-dresden.de/werkansicht/dlf/867/1/.

34. See Walter, "Fischer," in *New Grove Dictionary*, 895; Walter, "Fischer, in *Die Musik in Geschichte und Gegenwart*, col. 1254; and Walter, "Fischer," in *Lexikon zur deutschen Musikkultur*, cols. 636–37.

35. Dates given in Walter, *Fischer: Hofkapellmeister*, 247–48.

Fischer's title page offers the advice, "Magistris aeque ac Discipulis virtute et utilitate maxime commendandum" (Commended equally to skilled organists and to pupils in organ playing for their diligence and benefit). Similar phrases of musical aspiration are given by the elder Johann Speth on the title page of his *Ars magna consoni et dissoni*, published in Augsburg in 1693: "denen Instructoribus zum Vortheil; denen Lernenden aber zur sehr nutzlichen Ubung" (for the benefit of tutors, as well as for students as very useful exercises). A later example is found on the fair copy of Bach's *Well-Tempered Clavier*, Book 1: "Zum Nutzen und Gebrauch der Lehr-begierigen Musicalischen Jugend, als auch derer in diesem studio schon habil seyenden besonderem ZeitVertreib auffgesetzet" (For the use and profit of the musical youth desirous of learning as well as for the pastime of those already skilled in this study).[36] Despite their comparable aspirations, there are still differences among these three instances: Fischer and Speth published liturgical music for organ, while Bach, in contrast, compiled a manuscript tutor for stringed keyboard instruments. Speth, however, gives an instructive detail in his introductory advice: that is, to study the toccatas, preludes, and versets throughout on an unfretted clavichord.[37]

Successfully publishing didactic collections like *Ariadne Musica* required a clientele of wealthy experts or admirers who were able and willing to pay the higher cost for printed keyboard music. Bach's autograph, however, was primarily intended as a study score for his students (who still had to pay for their own copy)[38] and prepared them to play in all keys; it served (and continues to serve) as an "apex of his system of professional keyboard training, rather than for the delectation of amateurs."[39] However, the various transcriptions of Fischer's and Bach's collections (copied all or in part) are evidence of their position in the musical life of the time. Aside from this, we can recognize a difference from Bach in content: that is, Fischer's introduction to organ playing for the (Catholic) service, using different contrapuntal models, chorale

36. NBR, 97, no. 90.

37. "Sonsten habe diß alleinig anzufügen, daß zu rechter Bewerckstelligung diser Toccaten, Praeambulen, Versen &c. ein wohlzugerichtes und rein-gestimmtes Instrument oder Clavichordium erfordert werde, und zwar, daß dises letztere also zugericht seye, daß jedes Clavir seine eigene Seiten habe, und nicht etwan zwey, drey, biß 4. Clavir eine berühren." See Johann Speth, "Vorbericht," in *Ars magna consoni et dissoni*, 2nd ed (Augsburg: Lorenz Kroniger and Gottlieb Göbels Erben, 1702), accessed 29 January 2019, https://reader.digitale-sammlungen.de/de/fs1/object/display/bsb11187852_00006.html.

38. See Kirsten Beißwenger, "Rezeption und Verbreitung des Wohltemperierten Klaviers I zu Lebzeiten Johann Sebastian Bachs. Mit einem Exkurs über den Schreiber Anonymus Vr bzw. Anonymus 12 von Yoshitake Kobayashi," in *Bach. Das Wohltemperierte Klavier I. Tradition, Entstehung, Funktion, Analyse. Ulrich Siegele zum 70. Geburtstag*, ed. Siegbert Rampe, (München: Katzbichler, 2002), 7–25.

39. David Ledbetter, *Bach's Well-Tempered Clavier: The 48 Preludes and Fugues* (New Haven: Yale University Press, 2002), 15.

preludes, and a mixture of traditional and modern keys. The relationships between *Ariadne Musica* and *The Well-Tempered Clavier*—namely in the ascending order of the preludes—have repeatedly been discussed. Max Seiffert found additional relations between fugue subjects in the two collections: he posits Fischer's E-flat major fugue (FWV 40/2) as a model for Bach's Fugue in G Minor (BWV 861/2) (see Examples 1.1 and 1.2) and the tenor line of the E Phrygian prelude (FWV 41/1) as a model for the subject of Bach's Fugue in D Minor (BWV 539) (see Examples 1.3 and 1.4).[40] However, the relationship between FWV 40/2 and BWV 861/2 seems unconvincing to me. After a major second, Fischer's subject leaps down a minor seventh, followed by a stepwise rise of a diminished fifth; while Bach's subject, after an initial minor second, leaps a minor sixth, followed by deflection to a neighbor tone and, after an eighth rest, rises a minor third. A more reasonable possibility, instead, is that the subject of Bach's G-minor fugue was shaped from the fugato "Es ist der alte Bund," which begins in measure 131 of the second movement of Bach's cantata *Gottes Zeit ist die allerbeste Zeit* ("Actus tragicus," BWV 106) (see Example 1.5).

Inspired by Seiffert and Hohenemser, Reinhard Oppel published in the 1910 *Bach-Jahrbuch* some thoughts about Fischer's influence on Bach.[41] In eleven examples, he tried to show the importance of Fischer's keyboard works as a model for Bach's oeuvre. Among others, he detected a motivic analogy between Fischer's Praeludium VI in D Major (FWV 14), from *Les Pieces de Clavessin*, and Bach's Prelude in B-flat Major (BWV 866), from the first book of *The Well-Tempered Clavier* (see Examples 1.6 and 1.7). While this relationship is reasonable, in some other examples Oppel reached too far in his enthusiasm. For example, he proposed the unlikely relationship between the beginning of Fischer's Toccata (FWV 81), from the suite "Urania" in his *Musicalischer Parnassus*, and the opening of Bach's Prelude in B-flat Minor (BWV 867), in the first book of *The Well-Tempered Clavier* (see Examples 1.8 and 1.9).[42] And, contrary to another of Oppel's suggestions,[43] the beginning of the presto section in Fischer's Ouverture in G Major (FWV 74), from the suite "Calliope," is instead the core material for the beginning of Bach's Prelude in G Minor (BWV 808) in his English Suite, no. 3. Oppel's

---

40. Max Seiffert, *Geschichte der Klaviermusik. Die ältere Geschichte bis um 1750* (Leipzig: Breitkopf & Härtel, 1899; reprint, Hildesheim: Georg Olms, 1966), 230–31. Page references to this work are to the 1899 edition.

41. Reinhard Oppel, "Über Joh. Kasp. Ferd. Fischers Einfluß auf Joh. Seb. Bach," in BJ 7 (1910): 63–69 (quote on 64), accessed 29 January 2019, http://digital.slub-dresden.de/werkansicht/dlf/265293/71/o/.

42. Ibid., 64. Fischer's Toccata is published in von Werra, *Sämtliche Werke für Klavier und Orgel*, 65.

43. Oppel, "Über Fischers Einfluß," 65, example 4, erroneously described as beginning of Suite II in A Minor (BWV 807). Fischer's "Calliope" suite is published in von Werra, *Sämtliche Werke für Klavier und Orgel*, 39.

Example 1.1. J. C. F. Fischer, Fugue in E-flat Major
(FWV 40/2), from *Ariadne Musica*.

Example 1.2. J. S. Bach, Fugue in G Minor (BWV 861/2),
from *The Well-Tempered Clavier*, Book 1.

Example 1.3. J. C. F. Fischer, Prelude in E Phrygian
(FWV 41/1), from *Ariadne Musica*.

Example 1.4. J. S. Bach, Fugue in D Minor for Organ (BWV 539).

Example 1.5. J. S. Bach, "Es ist der alte Bund," from cantata
Gottes Zeit ist die allerbeste Zeit (BWV 106), mm. 131–34.

examples seem quite an overreach, because Bach finished the fair copy of his collection
in 1722, while Fischer's edition was published by Johann Christian Leopold (the son
of *Ariadne Musica*'s publisher) in Augsburg around 1738.[44] If we do not presume that
Fischer's manuscript was written in the first two decades of the eighteenth century
and that Bach had knowledge of it, the sequence Oppel suggested must be reversed.[45]

44. Gerber reports 1738 as the date of the print, though the edition is undated. Fischer dedicated it
to Princess Elisabeth Augusta of Baden-Baden, born March 16, 1726, "herself a well sophisticated
patron of music" ("Als einer selbst wohlerfahrnen und geneigten Music Patronin"). See "Fischer,
Johann Caspar Ferdinand," in Wessely, *Gerber: Neues historisch-biographisches Lexikon*, col. 135.

45. This topic was also neglected by Ichiro Sumikura in "Johann Sebastian Bach und Johann Kaspar
Ferdinand Fischer," in *Bericht über die wissenschaftliche Konferenz zum III. Internationalen Bach-Fest der
DDR. Leipzig, 18./19. September 1975*, ed. Werner Felix and Armin Schneiderheinze et. al. (Leipzig:
VEB Deutscher Verlag für Musik, 1977), 233–38.

Example 1.6. J. C. F. Fischer, Praeludium VI in D Major (FWV 14), from *Les Pieces de Clavessin*.

Example 1.7. J. S. Bach, Prelude in B-flat Major (BWV 866), from *The Well-Tempered Clavier*, Book 1.

Example 1.8. J. C. F. Fischer, Toccata (FWV 81), from Suite "Urania" in *Musicalischer Parnassus*.

Example 1.9. J. S. Bach, Prelude in B-flat Minor (BWV 867), from *The Well-Tempered Clavier*, Book 1.

On the other hand, nothing prevents us from assuming that Fischer obtained a copy of Bach's *Well-Tempered Clavier*, even though there is not a shadow to be found of Fischer's personal estate.

As mentioned above, Fischer organized his twenty preludes and fugues in a rising order, starting with C major (FWV 36), followed by C-sharp minor (FWV 37), D minor in Dorian key signature (FWV 38), and D major (FWV 39), and finishing with C minor (FWV 55) in Dorian key signature.[46] Finishing in the key of C minor means a return to the starting point, like mythic Theseus after finding his way out of the labyrinth. One may further note several contrasts to Bach's *Well-Tempered Clavier*. First, in Fischer's organization (beginning with FWV 38), preludes and fugues in minor keys are followed by pairs in major keys, while Bach's order is the opposite. Second, Fischer is not fully consistent in his order; in addition to starting in C major and finishing in C minor, there are three preludes based on E: that is, E Phrygian (FWV 41), E Dorian (FWV 42), and E major (FWV 43). In effect, he omits five keys from a fully chromatic order: C-sharp major, E-flat minor, F-sharp major, A-flat minor, and B-flat minor. In contrast, Bach's fair copy from 1722 is throughout chromatically ordered, starting with the C major prelude (BWV 846), followed by C minor (BWV 847), C-sharp major (BWV 848), C-sharp minor (BWV 849), and so on. Third, in some minor preludes, Fischer used the traditional Dorian key signature. Bach, however, did this only in some earlier versions, such as the Prelude in C Minor (BWV 847) in Wilhelm Friedemann's *Clavier-Büchlein*. In the case of Prelude and Fugue in A-flat Major (BWV 862), in a now-lost copy (which formerly belonged to the conductor Franz Konwitschny), Alfred Dürr made the fascinating discovery of numerous missing natural signs on the pitch D and, furthermore, the use of redundant B-flats. According to Dürr, these represent clear evidence of an original Lydian key signature, which Bach changed to a modern key signature, presumably while compiling the fair copy.[47] Fischer, however, also used the Lydian key signature in his Prelude XIV (FWV 49), in which the note D has a flatted accidental.[48]

---

46. On the organization of tonalities in *Ariadne Musica*, see Harold Powers, "From Psalmody to Tonality," in *Tonal Structures in Early Music*, ed. Cristle Collins Judd (New York: Garland, 1998), 275–340 (esp. 324–33). An instructive introduction to the topic is also given by Thomas Synofzik, "'Fili Ariadnaei': Entwicklungslinien zum Wohltemperierten Klavier," in Rampe, *Bach. Das Wohltemperierte Klavier I*, 109–46.

47. See "IV. Allgemeines, Präludium und Fuge As-Dur," in NBA V/6.1 (*Das Wohltemperierte Klavier I*, ed. Alfred Dürr; Kritischer Bericht, 1989), 189 and 362–64.

48. The use of accidental flats and the B-rotundum for cancellation, already used in *Les Pieces de Clavessin*, were praised by Tomáš Baltazar Janovka in his musical dictionary. See Tomáš Baltazar Janovka, "Chromatische signa," in *Clavis ad thesaurum magnae artis musicae* (Prague: Labaun, 1701), 12–15. In "Currens," 31–32, he quotes from *Les Pieces de Clavessin* and referred to this in "Einfall," 37–38, while in "Presto," 98, he recommends Fischer's *Les Pieces de Clavessin* in general. See also Synofzik, "'Fili Ariadnaei,'" 128–30.

At the end of the last Fugue in C Minor, Fischer adds the indication "Finis Praeludiorum" to mark the transition to the five ricercars, which are intended as a liturgical organ tutor. (Accordingly, in the present essay I do not analyze these five works—which, after all, appear after Fischer noted "Finis.") On the other hand, Fischer's note underscores the unity of each prelude and fugue; he indicates the pedal's use only in the preludes.[49] In the organs of the southern German-speaking countries as well as of Western Bohemia, the function of the pedal is quite different from those of Thuringia and Saxony, or Northern Germany. The first are fitted with mostly small pedals, disposed in a short range of ten to thirteen keys, which are not designated for the independent setting well known in Bach's organ works but instead more commonly used for pedal point and to reinforce cadences as well as final sections. Following this tradition, Fischer hints at only minimum technical requirements for the organist; however, skilled players are still able to use the pedal in fugues with rapid passagework, such as Fischer's D-major fugue (FWV 39/2). To be remembered is Speth's advice about playing his toccatas and preludes for organ also on a clavichord.

Bach, by contrast, wrote for stringed keyboard instruments and thereby widely relinquished use of the pedal. But in the final section of the A-minor fugue (BWV 865), for instance, a pedal would be helpful in playing the pedal point on A in measures 83–87. The use of a pedal harpsichord or clavichord was common in Bach's era, as well as in his lessons, because the useful pedal technique for the organ was taught on these instruments. Be that as it may, there is nothing to prevent us from playing *The Well-Tempered Clavier* on the clavichord, the harpsichord, or the organ—with or without the pedal.[50]

Looking to Fischer's fugue subjects, we can discover a variety of characters. Some are formed after older models that were commonly used in fugue setting and counterpoint studies of the sixteenth and seventeenth centuries. An example of such an archetype is the fugue subject in D major (FWV 39/2), with its characteristic repetitions on the note A, which aims at the F-sharp a third below, which in turn is the start of the following sixteenth-note figure (see Example 1.10). Models for a work might be assessed in different ways. Not more than an allusion for this D-major subject, for example, is the subject of the Canzon [III] in D Dorian by Matthias Weckmann, organist at St. Jacobi in Hamburg from 1655 to 1674.[51] Fischer's fugue subject, however, is instead

---

49. Fischer notates "Ped." in Preludes nos. 4, 6, 7, 10, 13, 16, 17, and 20, while in Preludes nos. 1, 15, 18, and 19 he notates "Ped. vel Man.," which means that here he leaves the use of the pedal to the player's discretion.

50. See Ledbetter, "Clavier," in *Bach's Well-Tempered Clavier*, 13–34.

51. Canzon in D is published in *Matthias Weckmann. Sämtliche freie Orgel- und Clavierwerke*, ed. Siegbert Rampe (Kassel: Bärenreiter, 2003), 35–37.

Example 1.10. J. C. F. Fischer, Fugue in D Major (FWV 39/2), from *Ariadne Musica*.

related to a subject in D major by Johann Pachelbel (see Examples 1.11 and 1.12).[52] The intervallic structure here is slightly different from Fischer's, but the common parts prevail. Unlike Pachelbel, the creator of the *Hexachordum Apollinis* (Nuremberg, 1699), Fischer composed from the subject a fugue in a single section of eighteen bars.

As mentioned above, Fischer used chorale incipits as fugue subjects, following the requirements of an organ tutor. In this context belongs the fugue subject in B minor (FWV 53/2), whose intervallic structure is related to the chorale "Herzlich thut mich erfreuen, / die liebe Sommerszeit," first published in a four-voice setting by Johann Walter in 1552 (see Examples 1.13 and 1.14).[53] Repeatedly examined elsewhere are Fischer's concise Prelude and Fugue in E Phrygian (FWV 41/1 and 41/2), which respectively occupy eleven measures (prelude) and eight measures (fugue) (see Examples 1.15 and 1.16).[54]

Consistent with the function of the prelude to anticipate what follows, Fischer assimilates the character of the subject in his prelude, whose beginning bears the nearly identical rhythm of the fugue. Fischer made the fugue's subject from Martin Luther's chorale incipit to "Aus tiefer Not schrei ich zu Dir," written on the text of Psalm 130 (Vulgate 129, "De profundis") in 1523.[55] The repeatedly used dissonant intervals and the augmented fifth, C–G-sharp (for example in measure 2 of the prelude), can be

52. Fugue in D Major is published in *Johann Pachelbel. Complete Works for Keyboard Instruments*, vol. 2, *Fugues*, ed. Michael Belotti, (Colfax, NC: Wayne Leupold, 2005), 9.

53. *Das deutsche Kirchenlied, Abteilung III:1, 1, Melodien aus Autorendrucken und Liedblättern. Notenband* (Kassel: Bärenreiter, 1993), 236–37, melody B 65. (Example 1.14 preserves the chorale's sixteenth-century orthography.)

54. For example, see Raymond Dittrich, "Bemerkungen zu Präludium und Fuge in e-Phrygisch aus Johann Caspar Ferdinand Fischers 'Ariadne Musica,'" *Musik und Kirche* 64 (1994): 83–86.

55. It is commonly overlooked that Luther had modeled the first line of his melody, with its characteristic fifth, after the beginning of the Marian song "Hilf, frau von Ach!" (Help, lady from Aachen), published in Erhart Oeglin's *Liederbuch* for four voices (Augsburg, 1512). See Robert Eitner and Julius Josef Maier, eds., *Erhart Oeglin's Liederbuch zu vier Stimmen. Augsburg 1512*, Publikation aelterer Praktischer und Theoretischer Musikwerke, vol. 9 (Berlin: T. Trautwein, 1880), 3–5, accessed 29 January 2019, http://www.columbia.edu/cu/lweb/digital/collections/cul/texts/ldpd_10276834_000/ldpd_10276834_000.pdf.

Example 1.11. M. Weckmann, Canzon in D Dorian.

Example 1.12. J. Pachelbel, Fugue in D Major.

Example 1.13. J. C. F. Fischer, Fugue in B Minor (FWV 53/2), from *Ariadne Musica*.

Hertz-lich thut mich er - frew - en, Die lie - be Som - mer - zeit,

Example 1.14. Chorale, "Herzlich thut mich erfreuen."

Example 1.15. J. C. F. Fischer, Prelude in E Phrygian (FWV 41/1),
from *Ariadne Musica*.

Example 1.16. J. C. F. Fischer, Fugue in E Phrygian (FWV 41/2),
from *Ariadne Musica*.

read as rhetorical figures, motivated by the chorale's first line of the following fugue. But why did he use this archaic mode in a collection based on modern keys? Is it indeed possible that Fischer wrote a fugue on this subject? He was a Catholic and a servant at a Catholic court—although Margrave Ludwig Wilhelm did grant a generous, liberal religious policy in the margravate of Baden in the Upper Rhine. Rudolf Walter suggests that Fischer used the subject to express a lament on his career, but Walter is silent about any further details.[56] More useful might be a closer look in the chorale's history. Psalm 130 is one of the penitential psalms, sung as part of vespers in the Catholic service as well as in the Lutheran. The year before *Ariadne Musica* was first published, Fischer published in Augsburg his collection of psalms for the vesper service of the liturgical year, titled *Vesperae seu Psalmi Vespertini*. In it, he also included this same psalm, impressively composed with four voices, two violins, and basso continuo, enhanced with ad libitum trombones and viols (FWV 32; see Example 1.17).[57] The setting begins with basso solo on the note F, followed by a descent of a minor third to D; through the octave jump upwards to d, he rises to b-flat and finishes the first line of text on the note a. In other words, he was not bound by Luther's Phrygian melody in composing this psalm but rather by interpreting the text.

The *Psalmi Vespertini* and *Ariadne Musica* are not strictly reserved for the Catholic Mass but also are usable for the Lutheran service. The simplest rationale regarding Fischer's use of the E Phrygian subject in his prelude and fugue could be the aim that *Ariadne Musica* be attractive to organists of both confessions. And this is all the more likely, since *Ariadne Musica* was self-published in 1702 and, quite rightly, Fischer was interested in good sales. But there may be a further possibility. By 1567, Luther's chorale had become common in Catholic hymnals with the text "Aus Herzens Grund schrei ich zu dir, / Herr Gott erhör mein stimme." In the first third of the seventeenth century, the same melody acquired the new text

> O Gütiger Gott in Ewigkeit,
> zu dir schreyt die gantze Christenheit,
> O Herr, O Gott gib Audientz, b'hüt uns vor Krieg und Pestilenz

which was sung as a prayer in Bohemia and Austria during the imperial wars against the Ottomans in the Balkans ever since the mid-seventeenth century.[58] Duke Julius

---

56. Walter, *Fischer. Hofkapellmeister*, 242.

57. Published in *Johann Caspar Ferdinand Fischer: Vesperpsalmen Opus III*, ed. Rudolf Walter, Das Erbe deutscher Musik, vol. 95 (Wiesbaden: Breitkopf & Härtel, 1991), 182–91.

58. See Wilhelm Bäumker, *Das katholische deutsche Kirchenlied in seinen Singweisen*, vol. 2 (Freiburg im Breisgau: Herder, 1883), 267–68; same text with another melody, 298 (no. 321), accessed 29 January 2019, https://reader.digitale-sammlungen.de/de/fs1/object/display/bsb11173437_00005.html.

Example 1.17. J. C. F. Fischer, Psalm 129 (130), "De profundis" (FWV 32), from *Psalmi Vespertini*, op. 3.

Franz of Saxe-Lauenburg and his son-in-law Margrave Ludwig Wilhelm (popularly called "Türkenlouis" by the last decade of the century)[59] were successful field commanders in the Ottoman wars, and in addition to material culture from the campaigns, they brought living spoils back to their countries. This, then, may also explain the appearance of such a subtext in Fischer's E Phrygian fugue.

In his compendium *Geschichte der Klaviermusik*, Max Seiffert included a clue to the origin of Fischer's fugue subject in F-sharp minor (FWV 46/2), suggesting that it stems from Johann Speth's *Magnificat primi toni*, where it appears as the subject of the second fugue (see Examples 1.18 and 1.19).[60] Fischer changed the key and modified the rhythm but retained the intervallic structure. Despite these changes, the origin of the subject remains quite recognizable for someone aware of the work. Using this composer's subject may be read as an expression of thanks for his support: in 1701 or 1702, Speth reported in a letter to the town council of Augsburg that he had been entrusted with the corrections in publishing Fischer's *Vesperae seu Psalmi Vespertini*, issued in 1701 by Lorenz Kroniger and Gottlieb Göbel's heirs.[61] The adoption of a fugue subject for such a reason was common in contrapuntal studies of that time and can be interpreted in different ways. While Fischer follows suit in modeling some fugue subjects that are more or less obvious in origin—for example, from such composers as Johann Jacob Froberger—he unveils for experts his scholarship as well as his contrapuntal skills in doing so. Yet it is impossible to recognize how he became acquainted with their music. Carl Philipp Emanuel Bach's report to Forkel in 1774 names Froberger as one of his father's admired composers; coincidence or not, Fischer shared this same admiration. The subject of his G-major fugue (FWV 48/2) is similar to the subject of Froberger's Capriccio in F (FbWV 516; see Examples 1.20 and 1.21).[62] And Fischer's fugue subject in A minor (FWV 50/2) shows an affiliation with one in Froberger's Fantasia V in A Minor (FbWV 205), but with marked changes (see Examples 1.22 and 1.23).[63]

According to Conrad Freyse, who served four decades as director of the Eisenach Bachhaus, Johann Ambrosius Bach possessed a hymnal, Dresden 1608; according to an editor's footnote in the following article, it contained the chorale "O Gütiger Gott in Ewigkeit" on p. 457. See Conrad Freyse, "Johann Sebastian Bachs erstes Gesangbuch," *Jahrbuch für Liturgik und Hymnologie* 6 (1961): 138–42 (quote on 138).

59. Hans Schmidt, "Ludwig Wilhelm," in *Neue Deutsche Biographie*, vol. 15 (1987), 350–54, accessed 29 January 2019, https://www.deutsche-biographie.de/pnd118729500.html#ndbcontent.

60. Seiffert, *Geschichte der Klaviermusik*, 231.

61. RISM A/I, F 985. The letter from Speth to the town council is given by Richard Schaal, "Zur Musikpflege im Kollegiatstift St. Moritz zu Augsburg," *Die Musikforschung* 7 (1954): 1–24 (esp. 9).

62. Froberger's Capriccio in F is published in Siegbert Rampe, ed., *Froberger. Neue Ausgabe sämtlicher Werke*, vol. 2 (Kassel: Bärenreiter, 1995), 46–49.

63. For Froberger's Fantasia V, see ibid., 40–41.

Example 1.18. J. C. F. Fischer, Fugue in F-sharp Minor (FWV 46/2),
from *Ariadne Musica*.

Example 1.19. J. Speth, *Magnificat primi toni*, verse 2,
from *Ars magna consoni et dissoni*.

Example 1.20. J. J. Froberger, Capriccio in F (FbWV 516).

Example 1.21. J. C. F. Fischer, Fugue in G Major (FWV 48/2),
from *Ariadne Musica*.

Example 1.22. J. J. Froberger, Fantasia V in A Minor (FbWV 205).

Example 1.23. J. C. F. Fischer, Fugue in A Minor (FWV 50/2),
from *Ariadne Musica*.

In contrast to Froberger's whole note and the following descending half notes after the octave a–a' (Example 1.22), Fischer starts not in the alto but in the tenor, with an anacrusis in diminished rhythm, repeating the note a three times and finishing with a neighbor-tone figure (Example 1.23). The connection with Froberger's subject exists in little more than its intervallic structure. However, Fischer's subject also quite strongly resembles the beginning of the second movement of Arcangelo Corelli's famous Sonata da chiesa a tre, op. 3, no. 4—which Bach, in turn, adapted in an organ transcription in B minor (BWV 579; see Examples 1.24 and 1.25).

Bach himself used, in a similar way, the subject from Fischer's four-part Fugue in F Major (FWV 45/2) for a three-part fugue in the first book of his *Well-Tempered Clavier* (BWV 856) (see Examples 1.26 and 1.27). He changed the meter from 3/4 to 3/8 and modified Fischer's dotted quarter-note rhythm to a running line of eighth and sixteenth notes. Although he slightly but markedly changed the intervals, he retained the (now) eighth-note upbeat as well as the subject's four-measure length. Fischer finished his dance-like *dux* with a falling fifth on a dotted half note before the *comes* enters, thereby effecting an interruption in the melodic flow. Bach, however, avoids this slowdown by continuing the line of sixteenth notes during the entrance of the *comes*.[64] Other differences, moreover, include the extent of the fugues: compare Fischer's thirty-four measures to the seventy-two measures of Bach's fugue, and consider Bach's more complex modulation scheme. Fischer uses only straightforward harmonic tonal relations, while Bach spiritedly goes further to achieve a wider range of harmonies. The aim of Bach's changes can be summarized as the development of a "Character-theme" or, in other words, a modification of rhythm and intervallic structure to create a characteristic subject.

Quite more complicated is the relationship between Fischer's subject in E major (FWV 43/2) and Bach's subject in the same key in the second book of *The Well-Tempered Clavier* (BWV 878; see Examples 1.28 and 1.29). In five measures, Fischer develops his subject in alla-breve meter, systematically rising from bass to soprano. As in his Fugue in F Major, he again uses the harmonic circle of E major with its relative major and minor. An older contrapuntal model for this same subject can be found in Johann Jacob Froberger's Ricercar IV in G Mixolydian (FbWV 404), but in common meter.[65] However, there are numerous contrapuntal works written since the fifteenth century that employ a similar subject: for example the Canon a 4 Voices, "Telluris ingens conditor," by John Bull,[66] but also the incipit of the chorale "O Jesu wahrer

---

64. See Ledbetter, *Bach's Well-Tempered Clavier*, 189–91.

65. Froberger's Ricercar IV is published in Rampe, *Froberger. Neue Ausgabe*, vol. 2, 96–97.

66. RISM ID no. 806336807, accessed 29 January 2019, https://opac.rism.info/search?id=806336807&View=rism.

Example 1.24. A. Corelli, Sonata da chiesa a tre,
op. 3, no. 4, second movement.

Example 1.25. J. S. Bach, Fugue in B Minor for organ,
after a theme by Corelli (BWV 579).

Example 1.26. J. C. F. Fischer, Fugue in F Major (FWV 45/2),
from *Ariadne Musica*.

Example 1.27. J. S. Bach, Fugue in F Major (BWV 856),
from *The Well-Tempered Clavier*, Book 1.

Example 1.28. J. C. F. Fischer, Fugue in E Major (FWV 43/2),
from *Ariadne Musica*.

Example 1.29. J. S. Bach, Fugue in E Major (BWV 878),
from *The Well-Tempered Clavier*, Book 2.

Gottes Sohn, / König im höchsten Thron," first published in 1531 by the "Böhmische Brüder"—particularly remarkable because of Fischer's own origin.[67] Finally, Alfred Dürr noted a similarity to the "Christe eleison" in the *Missa Pange lingua* by Josquin des Prez.[68] (See Examples 1.30–1.32.)

The subject of Bach's E-major fugue has the same meter sign and rising order of the four voices as in Fischer. In the subject's first half, Bach used the same progression, albeit noted in long-measured 4/2 time. In the subject's second part, he diminished Fischer's whole notes G-sharp and F-sharp to half notes. While Fischer, as in his subject of the F-major fugue, stops again to focus on the tonic e, Bach by contrast diminished this pitch to a quarter note and began the *comes* in the tenor line, giving the

67. See *Das deutsche Kirchenlied. Abteilung III:1, 3, Die Melodien aus Gesangbüchern II* (Kassel: Bärenreiter, 1998), 41, melody Eg 53. (Example 1.31 preserves the chorale's sixteenth-century orthography.)

68. Alfred Dürr, *Johann Sebastian Bach. Das Wohltemperierte Klavier* (Kassel: Bärenreiter, 1998), 312. Josquin des Prez, "Christe eleison," *Missa Pange lingua*, is published in *The Collected Works of Josquin des Prez*, ed. Willem Elders, vol. 4, *Masses Based on Gregorian Chants*, part 2 (Utrecht: Koninklijke Vereniging voor Nederlandse Muziekgeschiedenis, 2000), 2.

Example 1.30. J. J. Froberger, Ricercar IV (FbWV 404).

Example 1.31. Chorale, "O Jesu wahrer Gottes Sohn."

Example 1.32. Josquin des Prez, "Christe eleison,"
from *Missa Pange lingua*.

fugue a more consistent movement. In forty-three measures (according to the NBA),
Bach clearly expands the harmonic radius by modulating into B major and C-sharp
major. Or, in the words of David Schulenberg, Fischer, "working on a smaller scale,
had already begun using the theme in stretto, which Bach reserves for the following
section (mm. 9–16). This fugue is, then, an example of 'demonstration counterpoint,'
a new device being introduced after each cadence: a new type of stretto (m. 16), varied and diminuted forms of the subject (mm. 23, 27), combination of different forms
(mm. 30, 35)."[69] As noted by Christoph Wolff, these modifications became part of
the structure,[70] showing Bach's sophisticated skills in counterpoint, which are obvious in his development of nine different variations of the subject. At this point, Wolff
considered Bach's fugue closer to Froberger's ricercar than to Fischer's fugue.[71]

---

69. Schulenberg, *Keyboard Music of J. S. Bach*, 256.

70. Christoph Wolff, *Der stile antico in der Musik Johann Sebastian Bachs. Studien zu Bachs Spätwerk*,
Beihefte zum *Archiv für Musikwissenschaft* 6 (Wiesbaden: Franz Steiner, 1968), 61–66.

71. Ibid., 61. See also the smart observation of other works by Bach in Ledbetter, *Bach's Well-Tempered
Clavier*, 277–81.

In section V of his treatise *Gradus ad parnassum*, the imperial *Kapellmeister* Johann Joseph Fux used a subject modeled after Fischer's F-minor fugue (FWV 44/2) as an example for a "Fuga à 3. Modi A," followed by a second fugue that begins similarly to Froberger's ricercar with the note g' and with Fischer's meter, but diminished in the subject's second half, as in Bach (see Examples 1.33–1.35).[72] Could this be Bach's model? Because the model of Bach's E-major subject is quite common—or, more precisely, an archetype—we are not able to decide which model Bach used for BWV 878/2. The same is true with Bach's fugue subject in C-sharp minor (BWV 849/2) in the first book of *The Well-Tempered Clavier*. With five voices, this is one of the most sophisticated fugues that he composed and also is made with an archetype subject. Such a subject appears a minor second lower, in C minor and in common time, as the fugue subject for the "Crucifixus est" in the Credo of Fischer's *Missa Sancti Spiritus* (FWV 94), preserved in manuscript in the archive of the "Knights of the Cross with the Red Star" in Prague.[73] Seiffert found this subject also in a "Crucifixus del Sig. Kerll" (where it is titled "fugue"), in the appendix to the manuscript "Regulae Compositionis Musicae," and drew the parallel between Kerll's "Crucifixus" and Bach's Fugue in C-sharp Minor.[74] (See Examples 1.36–1.38.) Two years later, however, Adolf Sandberger became more specific in his introduction to the first volume of Kerll's collected works. He stated that Bach, with the subject in C-sharp minor, instead made a reference to Kerll's *Missa non sine quare*.[75]

As we return once more to the subject in E major (examined in Examples 1.28 and 1.29), it would be lovely to imagine the idea of a combination: Fischer's subject in E major as the younger composer's reference to the contrapuntal skills of the elder, together with Froberger's more bold harmonic constructions. But besides this imagi-

72. Johann Joseph Fux, *Gradus ad parnassum, sive manuductio ad compositionem musicae regularem* (Vienna: Johann Peter van Ghelen, 1725), 166–67.

73. *Johann Caspar Ferdinand Fischer: Missa Sancti Spiritus FWV 94*, ed. Hans Peter Eisenmann (Magdeburg: Edition Walhall-Verlag Franz Biersack, 1995), 33–34.

74. Seiffert, *Geschichte der Klaviermusik*, 389n1, gives the former shelf mark: D-B, Ms. theor. 4° 160. The actual shelf mark is Mus. ms. theor. 1480, fol. 33r-34r, according to Dr. Roland Schmidt-Hensel (D-B, Music Division) kind communication to author, 28 January 2019. Hermann Keller points to this subject but without reference to Seiffert or to the Berlin manuscript. See Hermann Keller, *Das Wohltemperierte Klavier von Johann Sebastian Bach. Werk und Wiedergabe* (Kassel: Bärenreiter, 1965), 53; Keller, *The Well-Tempered Clavier by Johann Sebastian Bach*, trans. Leigh Gerdine (London: George Allen & Unwin, 1976), 62.

75. Adolf Sandberger, ed., *Ausgewählte Werke von Johann Kaspar Kerll. Erster Theil*, Denkmäler Deutscher Tonkunst. Zweite Folge: Denkmäler der Tonkunst in Bayern, II/2 (Leipzig: Breitkopf & Härtel, 1901), xlvii, accessed 29 January 2019, http://daten.digitale-sammlungen.de/0006/bsb00064299/images/index.html?id=00064299&groesser=&fip=193.174.98.30&no=&seite=49.

Example 1.33. J. C. F. Fischer, Fugue in F Minor (FWV 44/2),
from *Ariadne Musica*.

Fuga à 3. Modi A.

Example 1.34. J. J. Fux, Fuga à 3 (Modi A.),
from *Gradus ad parnassum*, section V, chapter III.

Fuga à 3. Modi C.

Example 1.35. J. J. Fux, Fuga à 3 (Modi C.),
from *Gradus ad parnassum*, section V, chapter III.

Example 1.36. J. S. Bach, Fugue in C-sharp Minor (BWV 849/2),
from *The Well-Tempered Clavier*, Book 1.

Example 1.37. J. C. F. Fischer, "Crucifixus,"
from *Missa Sancti Spiritus* (FWV 94), mm. 78–84.

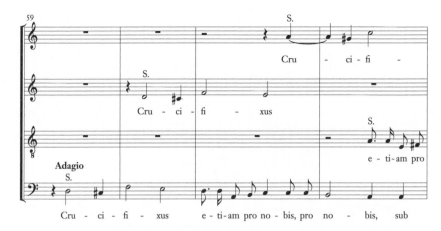

Example 1.38. J. C. Kerll, "Crucifixus,"
from *Missa non sine quare*, mm. 59–62.

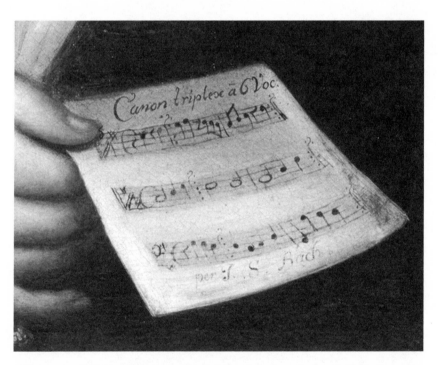

Figure 1.3. J. S. Bach, *Canon triplex à 6 Voc:* (BWV 1076), detail of the portrait
by Elias Gottlob Haussmann, Leipzig, 1748. Bach-Archiv Leipzig (BS 12).
Reproduced with permission.

nation, one sees that the E major subject must have been important for Bach in his last decade. Only a short time after compiling the second book of *The Well-Tempered Clavier* (London autograph), he invited the viewer of his portrait, painted by Elias Gott-lob Haussmann in 1746 and 1748, to solve his enigmatic *Canon triplex à 6 Voc:* (BWV 1076; see Figure 1.3).[76] Notated in tenor clef, the middle voice contains the formerly E major subject, but adjusted for the new context. The rather sophisticated exercise reveals Bach as a learned musician with extraordinary knowledge in counterpoint, showing experts his possibilities for the elaboration of such an all-purpose subject.

Conclusion

The relationship between Johann Caspar Ferdinand Fischer and Johann Sebastian Bach is still evident in the tonal order of *Ariadne Musica* and *The Well-Tempered Clavier*. By contrast, Bach's adoption of fugue subjects does not appear as a one-to-one correspon-dence to the model but rather more as a creative act, expressed by characteristic changes in the meter, note values, or rhythm. The hypotheses devised, therefore, in evaluating this artful act are manifold and, in the end, possibly insignificant. The closer look at the inner context of Fischer's *Ariadne Musica* and his contrapuntal involvement with older models—such as those of Johann Jacob Froberger or Johann Pachelbel, together with their reworking—unveils insights into his own musical tradition and perhaps his education. Viewed in light of his historical and biographical environment, we can see influences present in his *Ariadne Musica* that, until now, have only been sensed beneath the surface but were elusive analytically. The differences in the aim of Fischer's and Bach's collections are clearly recognizable, despite their common features. Be that as it may, an intense engagement with Fischer's keyboard works on their own terms is profitable in every way, from a musicological aspect and also in musical practice.

76. The canon on this painting is also available as a copperplate etching. For details, see NBA VIII/1 (*Kanons, Musikalisches Opfer*, ed. Christoph Wolff; Kritischer Bericht, 1976), 40.

Repaying Debt with Interest

The Revision of Borrowed Movements
in C. P. E. Bach's Passions

Moira Leanne Hill

*Borrowing is allowed; one must however repay what is borrowed
with interest, that is, one must arrange and elaborate the copy such
that it gains a more beautiful and improved appearance than the
setting from which it was borrowed.*[1]
—Johann Mattheson, *Der vollkommene Capellmeister*, 1739

The phenomenon of composers arranging and performing the works of fellow composers has generally received less consideration than original compositions have from scholars of music history. Nevertheless, abundant instances exist in which eighteenth-century composers furnished the music of their predecessors or contemporaries with such "improvements." For example, Johann Sebastian Bach adapted Giovanni Battista Pergolesi's *Stabat Mater* in his *Tilge, Höchster, meine Sünden*, BWV 1083, providing it with a new German text, an augmented orchestration, and an independent viola line. Bach fashioned this adaptation in the 1740s, the same decade in which he arranged Gottfried Heinrich Stölzel's aria "Dein Kreuz, o Bräutgam meiner Seelen" from his Passion oratorio *Ein Lämmlein geht und trägt die Schuld* (1720). Bach parodied Stölzel's model by furnishing it with a new text, and he also altered its musical setting through transposition, new instrumentation, and even recomposition. The resulting aria, "Bekennen will ich seinen Namen," BWV 200, is thought to have appeared in a cantata that is now lost.[2] J. S. Bach's contemporary George Frideric Handel integrated portions of a printed collection of Franz Johann Habermann's masses from 1747 into his oratorio *Jephtha* (1751), one of myriad instances in which

---

1. "Entlehnen ist eine erlaubte Sache; man muss aber das Entlehnte mit Zinsen erstatten, d. i. man muss die Nachahmungen so einrichten und ausarbeiten, daß sie ein schöneres und besseres Ansehen gewinnen als die Sätze, aus welchen sie entlehnet sind."

2. Peter Wollny, "'Bekennen will ich seinen Namen'-Authentizität, Bestimmung und Kontext der Arie BWV 200. Anmerkungen zu Johann Sebastian Bachs Rezeption von Werken Gottfried Heinrich Stölzels," BJ 94 (2008): 123–58.

Handel arranged and incorporated—some have argued plagiarized—other composers' works into his own.[3] In each case, both the choice of musical model and the particular methods of revision reveal something about the composer who undertook this project, such as whose music he held in esteem, what the requisite performing conditions were, and how his own aesthetic preferences or stylistic goals differed from those of the original work's composer.

This phenomenon of taking and adapting the works of others was not exclusive to the generation of J. S. Bach and Handel. This essay examines its occurrence in works by a member of the following generation with connections to both figures, Carl Philipp Emanuel Bach. Specifically, it analyzes the procedures he used to alter and transform existing musical material and texts for their incorporation into his twenty-one liturgical settings of the Passion story, focusing on those borrowed *accompagnati*, arias, choruses, and occasionally duets that were added, along with chorales, to the literal biblical narratives of his Passion settings.

For Bach, the process of borrowing materials for use in the Passions often involved a considerable amount of creative input, as an investigation into his alterations to both the texts and the musical settings of these loaned movements shows. Understanding the likely reasons behind his decisions leads to a fuller appreciation of the sensitivity with which he worked and the extent to which he often went beyond that which was strictly necessary to make borrowed material function in its new context. Indeed, a variety of motivations underlies these modifications, as suggested below. Clear patterns of parody and revision emerge, based on such factors as the genre of the original work or the musical style of a borrowed movement, which naturally correlates strongly to who composed it.

Ultimately, how Bach altered his borrowed movements over the course of his two decades in Hamburg is consistent with a broad move away from musical and textual idioms of the baroque. For the setting of parody texts, this entails updating the poetry of the previous generation to reflect more contemporary language and theological ideas. In the musical settings, Bach increasingly obscures or eliminates the da capo formal structure from many borrowed movements by truncating major portions of them. In addition, he substantially revised the melodies of many movements, at times making them more lyrical and singable through the greater use of stepwise motion or by simplifying melodic or rhythmic elements. His manner of applying parody texts to existing music also favored more natural, speech-like features, such as syllabic text setting and less frequent repetition of single words and short phrases. Thus, both textual parody and musical revision evince Bach's developing aesthetic values.

3. Max Seiffert, "Franz Johann Habermann (1706–1783)," *Kirchenmusikalisches Jahrbuch* 18 (1903): 81–94.

This study is divided into two parts: a discussion of methods and motivations for textual revision and a corresponding discussion of methods and motivations for musical changes, with particular consideration of text-setting issues in cases when Bach furnished an alternate text. This bifurcated structure draws parallels between the composer's treatment of texts and music, as arguably both reflect the same basic drive to refine, update, and make borrowed material his own.

Six groups consisting of model movements together with their various versions crafted by Bach for his Hamburg Passion settings will illustrate the composer's varied approaches toward revision. In four of the groups studied, a model movement spawned two instances of borrowing. In such cases, both could be derived independently from the original model, or the second version could emerge from Bach's prior reworking of the model (a so-called secondary borrowing). In at least one instance studied below, the composer even consulted both the original and his own prior version in fashioning yet another variant of a borrowed movement. Parody procedure, in which a new or heavily updated text supplants the original, plays a role in each group of examples.

The movements in these six groups of examples span the years that Bach wrote Passions in Hamburg. One group, based on the tenor aria "Verdammt ihn nur, ihr ungerechten Richter" from Gottfried August Homilius's *St. Mark Passion* (HoWV I.10, no. 23), includes Bach's early version with the same text from his own 1770 *St. Mark Passion* (no. 13), as well as his late parodied and heavily revised version "Erfrecht euch nur, die Unschuld zu verklagen" from the 1789 *St. Matthew Passion* (no. 19). A second group encompasses two versions of Stölzel's aria "Liebste Hand! ich küsse dich" from that composer's Passion oratorio *Sechs geistliche Betrachtungen* (1741), which Bach adapted for his 1772 *St. John Passion* using the same text (no. 5), and parodied seven years later (1779 *St. Luke Passion*, no. 4) with a text that begins "Ach, dass wir Erbarmung fünden." A third group of examples, inspected here only for their texts, concerns another aria from Homilius's *St. Mark Passion*, "Mensch, empfinde doch Erbarmen" (no. 3); Bach parodied this for use in 1772 ("So freiwillig, ohne Klage," no. 15), and then again for his 1780 *St. John Passion* ("Um in Schwachheit mich zu stärken," no. 17). Two groups of movements are examined only for textual alterations: group four comprises J. S. Bach's chorus "Ruht wohl, ihr heiligen Gebeine," from his *St. John Passion* (BWV 245, no. 67), along with C. P. E. Bach's version from 1772 (no. 23), featuring altered poetry; group five considers the model aria "Vor Dir, dem Vater, der verzeiht" from Homilius's *St. John Passion* (HoWV I.4, no. 16) and includes both Bach's use of it in his 1774 *St. Mark Passion* (no. 15, same title) and his parodied version from 1789 (no. 14, "Im Staub gebückt"). Benda's aria "Droht nur, ihr Gefahren," from his cantata *Ihr brausenden Wogen, bestürmet die Lüfte* (L 518), and Bach's parody of it, "Die Unschuld wird verfolgt," made for the 1784 *St. John Passion* (no. 12), constitute the sixth group studied in this essay. Before we investigate these movements, however, an overview of

Bach's output of sacred music while he lived in Hamburg—with particular attention to the role of borrowing and arrangement in liturgical music in general, and especially in his Passion settings—provides a useful context.

Bach moved from Berlin to Hamburg in 1768 to assume the position of cantor and music director for the five main churches in that city. A requirement of this post was to provide music for liturgical and some nonliturgical occasions throughout the year. A substantial portion of Bach's resulting works for his office comprises three groups: liturgical cantatas, including both simple ones for regular Sundays and grand ones known as *Quartalsmusiken* intended for four larger feast days spread throughout the year; occasional cantatas celebrating the installation of new pastors; and an annual Passion that was heard on Sundays in Lent at Hamburg's larger churches.

Bach's methods for providing the necessary music varied. Some of these works he composed from scratch. Other obligatory performances featured existing works composed by others or from his own prior output, which could be adapted to and arranged for the occasion. Other works were fashioned by pasting together movements from different origins, a technique known as pasticcio. In constructing pasticcios, Bach had the option to assemble such works entirely from borrowed material or to incorporate contributions that had been newly composed for the occasion.

Examples of borrowing and pasticcio are not difficult to find in Bach's Hamburg output. For example, the opening chorus of his Easter cantata *Jauchzet, frohlocket, auf, preiset die Tage*, Wq 242 (H 804; BR-CPEB Fp 9), presented to Hamburg congregations in 1778, is none other than the famous first movement of his father's *Christmas Oratorio*, BWV 248—itself a chorus that Johann Sebastian had borrowed and parodied from his own secular cantata *Tönet, ihr Pauken! Erschallet, Trompeten!*, BWV 214. Philipp Emanuel's Wq 242 also takes movements from works by Carl Heinrich Graun and Gottfried August Homilius, gluing these together with recitatives newly composed for the occasion.[4] Comparable examples can also be found in the pastoral installation cantatas.[5] In the Passions, the proportion of borrowed and new material could vary considerably from Passion to Passion.[6] For example, his first Passion, performed in

4. See CPEB:CW, V/2.1, *Quartalsstücke I*, ed. Mark W. Knoll (Los Altos, Calif.: Packard Humanities Institute, 2015), xx, 246, 248, and commentary. For a study of borrowing and parody in the *Quartalsmusiken*, see Clemens Harasim, *Die Quartalsmusiken von Carl Philipp Emanuel Bach: Ihre Quellen, ihre Stilistik und die Bedeutung des Parodieverfahrens* (Marburg: Tectum, 2010).

5. A summary of borrowing and pasticcio in the pastoral installation cantatas is found in Wolfram Enßlin and Uwe Wolf, "Die Prediger-Einführungsmusiken von C. P. E. Bach. Materialien und Überlegungen zu Werkbestand, Entstehungsgeschichte und Aufführungspraxis," BJ 93 (2007): 139–78. The installation cantatas are published in CPEB:CW, series V.

6. Refer to the individual entries for each Passion in BR-CPEB. This same information plus much more can be found in the individual volumes of CPEB:CW, series IV.

1769, and his penultimate Passion from 1788 included much material composed expressly for those occasions. His Passions from 1770 and 1775, however, each feature mostly a single borrowed work—settings of Mark and Luke Passions by his contemporary Homilius in Dresden. Indeed, these can be designated as arrangements of their respective models. In other Passions, Bach mixed together movements pulled from as many as five composers.

Of all the genres in which Bach worked in his role as Hamburg's music director, the single largest block is formed by the Passions, as is evident by browsing through the catalog of the composer's estate published in 1790.[7] They present the perfect body of works for case studies on a variety of topics, not only because so many examples exist from this one genre but also because all were produced under the same requirements over the entire span of Bach's Hamburg tenure—two decades in all, with a resulting total of twenty-one Passions. Hamburg tradition stipulated that the works rotate sequentially through setting the narratives of the Evangelists Matthew, Mark, Luke, and John, respectively, over a four-year cycle; that the performance of each work last roughly an hour; and that each Passion be new to the congregation, which is to say not a repetition of one previously heard. All of Bach's Passions conformed to these traditions.

When comparing these similar works to each other with an eye on Bach's borrowing practices, conspicuous patterns emerge. After borrowing and adapting musical settings of the Passion narrative toward the beginning of his tenure, the composer often reused these as well as many of the accompanying chorales in subsequent settings of the same Evangelist. These building blocks for the narrative and many of the chorales were derived from his father's *St. Matthew Passion*, three Passions by Homilius, and two Passions by his predecessor in Hamburg, Georg Philipp Telemann. In contrast, the other movements inserted into the narrative—that is, the *accompagnati*, arias, duets, and choruses, whose texts were usually free poetry—seldom reappeared. This gave the Passions a certain freshness from year to year and from cycle to cycle. By replacing these interpolations, even while retaining narratives and chorales that had been heard before, his Passions could be considered "new" while still containing material borrowed from previous years and cycles.

These non-chorale interpolations came roughly in three varieties—borrowed, arranged, or newly composed for the occasion (see Table 2.1).[8] The borrowed ones were movements taken from Passions or cantatas written by his contemporaries or

---

7. *Verzeichniß des musikalischen Nachlasses des verstorbenen Capellmeisters Carl Philipp Emanuel Bach* (Hamburg, 1790).

8. Information in Table 2.1 is drawn from CPEB:CW, series IV, and BR-CPEB. (When movement nos. occasionally differ between CPEB:CW and BR-CPEB, Table 2.1 follows CPEB:CW.) Column 4 ("Song Arrangements") is based in part on Table 1 in Moira Leanne Hill, "Die Lied-Ästhetik

Table 2.1. Summary of borrowings in C. P. E. Bach's Passions (excluding biblical narrative and chorales)

Year (H no.)	Borrowed from Other Composers	Self-Borrowed	Song Arrangements	Newly Composed
1769 (H 782)	chorus no. 36 (BWV 245/40^{II})	chorus no. 2 (Wq 215/4, 1st version)		12 movements later incorporated into Wq 233
1770 (H 783)	aria no. 7 (HoWV I.10/15) aria no. 13 (HoWV I.10/23) aria no. 17 (HoWV I.10/30) accomp.–aria–accomp. no. 21 (HoWV I.10/34) aria no. 27 (HoWV I.10/40) aria no. 29 (HoWV I.10/42)			
1771 (H 784)	chorus no. 1 (L 540/1) aria–recit.–aria–accomp. no. 2 (L 540/5) duet no. 5 (Stölzel, I. Betrachtung, no. 5) aria no. 7 (Stölzel, III. Betrachtung, no. 5) duet no. 11 (Stölzel, III. Betrachtung, no. 3) aria no. 19 (Stölzel, V. Betrachtung, no. 3) aria–chorus no. 21 (HoWV I.10/9) chorus no. 23 (HoWV I.10/48)			
1772 (H 785)	aria no. 5 (Stölzel, II. Betrachtung, no. 3) aria no. 9 (HoWV I.10/25) aria no. 11 (Stölzel, IV. Betrachtung, no. 5) aria no. 15 (HoWV I.10/3)* chorus no. 17 (Stölzel, VI. Betrachtung, no. 3) duet no. 21 (Stölzel, VI. Betrachtung, no. 5)* chorus no. 23 (BWV 245/67)*			

Year (H no.)	Borrowed from Other Composers	Self-Borrowed	Song Arrangements	Newly Composed
1773 (H 786)	chorus no. 2 (HoWV II.49/1)			
	accomp. no. 3 (HoWV II.49/2)			
	accomp. no. 7 (HoWV I.9/6)			
	aria no. 8 (HoWV I.9/7)			
	aria no. 10 (HoWV I.9/13)			
	aria no. 15 (HoWV I.9/17)			
	accomp. no. 19 (HoWV I.9/20)			
	aria no. 20 (HoWV I.9/21)			
	aria no. 26 (HoWV I.9/24)			
	aria no. 28 (HoWV I.9/30)			
1774 (H 787)	chorus no. 2 (HoWV I.9/8)			
	aria no. 6 (HoWV I.9/10)			
	accomp. no. 14 (HoWV I.4/15)			
	aria no. 15 (HoWV I.4/16)			
	accomp. no. 17 (HoWV I.4/20)			
	aria no. 18 (HoWV I.4/21)			
	aria no. 21 (HoWV I.4/25)			
	aria no. 25 (HoWV I.4/37)			
	chorus no. 29 (HoWV I.5/44)			
1775 (H 788)	aria no. 5 (HoWV I.5/18)			
	aria–accomp.–aria no. 7 (HoWV I.5/20)			
	aria no. 11 (HoWV I.5/24)			
	aria no. 17 (HoWV I.5/31)			
	trio no. 19 (HoWV I.5/33)			
	accomp.–chorus–accomp. no. 25 (HoWV I.5/39)			
	chorus no. 26 (HoWV I.5/40)			

Year (H no.)	Borrowed from Other Composers	Self-Borrowed	Song Arrangements	Newly Composed
1776 (H 789)	aria–accomp.–aria no. 5 (HoWV I.4/5) aria no. 9 (HoWV I.4/9) aria no. 11 (HoWV I.4/11) aria no. 19 (HoWV I.4/27) aria no. 21 (HoWV I.4/29) duet no. 25 (HoWV I.4/33)			1 arioso (no. 16a), 1 accomp. (no. 28)
1777 (H 790)	chorus no. 4 (L 528/1) chorus no. 12 (L 523/1) aria no. 16b (GraunWV B:III:29)* aria no. 24 (HoWV II.49/3)	aria no. 8 (H 821a/3) aria no. 20 (H 821a/5)* aria no. 29 (H 821a/13)*	chorus no. 2 (Wq 194/14)	
1778 (H 791)	aria no. 5 (HoWV I.5/14) aria no. 9 (HoWV I.5/8) chorus no. 13 (HoWV I.9/19) duet no. 17 (HoWV I.5/12) aria no. 21 (HoWV I.9/4) accomp. no. 23 (HoWV I.9/26) chorus no. 28 (L 515/1)* accomp. no. 31 (HoWV I.9/29)		*chorus no. 24 (H 790/2)*	
1779 (H 792)	chorus no. 1 (HoWV I.4/39) aria no. 24 (L 515/3)*	aria no. 4 (H 785/5)* aria no. 7 (H 821g/7)* aria no. 11 (H 821g/5)* aria no. 19 (H 821h/5)* aria no. 22 (H 821c/3)*		2 accomp. (nos. 6 and 21)
1780 (H 793)	aria no. 6 (L 516/3)* aria no. 10 (L 516/5)* aria no. 13 (GraunWV A:III:4, no. 2)* aria no. 21 (L 564/3)* chorus no. 25 (HoWV I.4/18)*	aria no. 17 (H 785/15)*	*chorus no. 2 (H 790/2)*	1 accomp. (no. 12)

Year (H no.)	Borrowed from Other Composers	Self-Borrowed	Song Arrangements	Newly Composed
1781 (H 794)	chorus no. 2 (HoWV II.72/1) aria no. 7 (L 565/3)* aria no. 9 (L 565/5)	aria no. 26 (H 821i/6)*	chorus no. 14 (Wq 196/9) chorus no. 16 (Wq 196/13) chorus no. 20 (Wq 194/23) chorus no. 28 (Wq 197/6)	2 accomp. (nos. 6 and 19)
1782 (H 795)	aria no. 13 (L 540/3) aria no. 22 (L 575/3)*		chorus no. 7 (Wq 198/29) chorus no. 17 (Wq 198/26) chorus no. 28 (Wq 198/6) chorus no. 30 (Wq 197/13)	1 accomp. (no. 21)
1783 (H 796)	aria no. 19 (L 547/1)*		chorus no. 3 (H 794/20) chorus no. 13 (Wq 196/30) chorus no. 21 (Wq 196/23) chorus no. 27 (Wq 198/15)	2 accomp. (nos. 5 and 8), 2 arias (nos. 6 and 9)
1784 (H 797)	aria no. 5 (L 527/5)* aria no. 12 (L 518/5)*		chorus no. 9 (Wq 202/E/6) chorus no. 17 (H 790/2) chorus no. 19 (Wq 198/23)	2 accomp. (nos. 11 and 16), 1 aria (no. 23)
1785 (H 798)		chorus no. 27 (Wq 215/4, 2nd version)*	chorus no. 2 (Wq 198/4) chorus no. 13 (Wq 197/21) chorus no. 17 (H 794, no. 16)	1 accomp. (no. 4), 1 arioso (no. 21), 3 arias (nos. 5, 9, 25)
1786 (H 799)			chorus no. 5 (Wq 198/3) aria–chorus no. 13 (Wq 197/3) chorus no. 17 (H 795/17) aria no. 21b (Wq 198/28) aria no. 23 (Wq 198/11)	1 accomp. (no. 21a), 2 arias (no. 9 and 27)

Year (H no.)	Borrowed from Other Composers	Self-Borrowed	Song Arrangements	Newly Composed
1787 (H 800)			aria no. 4 (Wq 194/21) aria no. 16 (Wq 198/21)	2 arias (nos. 10 and 18), aria–accomp.–chorus (no. 6), 2 choruses (nos. 2 and 20)
1788 (H 801)				1 accomp. (no. 21), 5 arias (nos. 5, 9, 11, 17, 22), 2 choruses (nos. 15 and 24)
1789 (H 802)	aria no. 6 (HoWV I.4/5)* aria no. 9 (HoWV I.4/9)* aria no. 14 (HoWV I.4/16)* aria no. 19 (HoWV I.10/23)*	chorus nos. 2 and 27 (Wq 204) accomp. no. 18 (H 786, no. 7) aria no. 25 (H 786, no. 8)		1 accomp. (no. 8)

Note: Pieces with parody texts are indicated with an asterisk (*). Reuses of song arrangements' musical settings are indicated with italics.

by members of the preceding generation. Sometimes Bach left these untouched, and other times he changed their text and music to some degree, this latter phenomenon being the central focus of this essay. The arranged interpolations were arrangements of his own sacred songs, originally for solo voice and keyboard. He transformed these domestic songs into arias or choruses by adding an instrumental ensemble accompaniment and, in the case of the choruses, three voices below the melody.[9] The newly composed interpolations were those movements—which could include *accompagnati*, arias, and choruses—written expressly for a given Passion.

Over the twenty years that Bach worked in Hamburg, the sources for the *accompagnati*, ariosos, arias, and choruses interpolated into the narratives of his Passions evolved as he generally shifted from relying on borrowings to crafting song arrangements to composing new movements for the occasion (see Table 2.2).[10] Excepting his *St. Matthew Passion* of 1769—Bach's first foray into the genre and part of his effort to establish himself as a respected composer of large-scale sacred music—the works featured borrowings most heavily through the year 1781. Song arrangements appeared most frequently in the Passions from 1781 to 1786 or 1787, and new contributions constitute large parts of the works from 1783 to 1788. Bach died in 1788, and the reason his final contribution to this genre, prepared at the end of his life, reverted to borrowings was almost certainly due to infirmity in old age.

---

in Carl Philipp Emanuel Bachs späten Passionen," in *Carl Philipp Emanuel Bach im Spannungsfeld zwischen Tradition und Aufbruch: Beiträge der interdisziplinären Tagung anlässlich des 300. Geburtstages von Carl Philipp Emanuel Bach vom 6. bis 8. März 2014 in Leipzig*, ed. Christine Blanken and Wolfram Enßlin, Leipziger Beiträge zur Bachforschung 12 (Hildesheim: Olms, 2016), 80.

9. Bach's song arrangements are excluded from this discussion, as their preparation involved procedures that differed from most of the revision techniques examined in this essay. For a discussion of these movements, see Hill, "Die Lied-Ästhetik," 79–94; see also Wolfram Enßlin, "Formen der Selbstrezeption. Carl Philipp Emanuel Bachs Umarbeitungen Zahlreicher Sololieder zu Chören," in *Kultur- Und Musiktransfer im 18. Jahrhundert: Das Beispiel C.P.E. Bach in musikkultureller Vernetzung Polen-Deutschland-Frankreich. Bericht über das Internationale Symposium vom 5. bis 8. März 2009 in Frankfurt (Oder) und Wrocław*, ed. Hans-Günter Ottenberg (Frankfurt/Oder: Musikgesellschaft Carl Philip Emanuel Bach, 2010), 55–95.

10. In Table 2.2, movements given the same number designation in the published editions of CPEB:CW and (for forthcoming volumes) in BR-CPEB are typically counted as a single interpolation. However, an exception is made if these two movements have a fundamentally different origin (e.g., 1786: 21a is a newly-composed *accompagnement* while 21b is an aria arranged by C. P. E. Bach from one of his songs). If a movement's musical setting is repeated in the same Passion (e.g., choruses in the 1787 and 1789 Passions), these are counted as two interpolations. Column 1 does not include song arrangements.

Table 2.2. Types of models for non-chorale interpolations
in C. P. E. Bach's Passions

	Borrowings	Song Arrangements	New Compositions
1769	2		12
1770	6		
1771	8		
1772	7		
1773	10		
1774	9		
1775	7		
1776	6		
1777	7	1	2
1778	8	1	
1779	7		2
1780	6	1	1
1781	4	4	2
1782	2	4	1
1783	1	4	4
1784	2	3	3
1785	1	3	5
1786		5	3
1787		2	5
1788			8
1789	8		1

The fact that borrowings featured most prominently in the first half of Bach's Hamburg tenure and again right at the end as he suffered from failing health does seem to suggest that he borrowed to reduce the work associated with writing his annual Passion. His position in Hamburg required him to provide music for more than two hundred occasions each year, and he similarly used both wholesale borrowing and pasticcio technique for occasional and regular liturgical cantatas as well. The decision to borrow in these genres makes sense, as these were not works that would be published or reused in their entirety.

As summarized in Table 2.1, an examination of the sources for the borrowed interpolations (excluding the chorales) reveals that these overwhelmingly come from Passions or cantatas written by his contemporaries and by members of the preceding generation, or from works by Bach himself. More specifically, the origins of these movements included his father's *St. John Passion* and *St. Matthew Passion*; a Passion oratorio from his father's contemporary in Gotha, Gottfried Heinrich Stölzel; three liturgical Passions, a Passion oratorio, and two cantatas by Homilius; a whole stash of cantatas by Stölzel's successor, Georg Anton Benda, that Bach had on hand; two secular Italian cantatas by Carl Heinrich Graun and Johann Gottlieb Graun in Berlin; and his own cantatas written for the installation of Hamburg pastors, which sometimes included his own compositions but could also feature material by others that he had adapted for the occasion. Bach also borrowed from his own Magnificat and from his settings of the old and new Litanies, and occasionally even from his own Passions.

When one examines the entire body of borrowed interpolated arias, choruses, *accompagnati*, and similar movements from Bach's liturgical Passions—tracing origins and types of models over the course of the twenty years during which these works were created—clear trends emerge. Bach's heaviest borrowing was from works by his Dresden contemporary Homilius, followed by Benda's cantatas, Stölzel's Passion, his own pastoral installation cantatas, and then from other assorted remaining works (see Table 2.3).[11] Not only do borrowed interpolations in the Passions tend to be prevalent during the first half of his Hamburg tenure, but even within these years Bach's reliance on a single composer or source type (like his installation cantatas) tends to cluster into discrete time periods.

Focusing now on Bach's annual Passions—specifically on the interpolated movements, excepting the chorales—the next questions that logically follow are these: What did Bach change? How exactly did he accomplish this adaptation? And why might he have done so? It is useful to begin simply by examining Bach's modifications to his texts.

Changes to the Text

Bach preserved the original texts for many of the interpolations that he adopted from existing sources for use in his Hamburg Passions.[12] However, for a significant number of such movements, he opted to change them in ways that suggest his sensitivity to such concerns as how they suited their narrative position, how modern or antiquated their poetic language was, whether they conformed to more recent currents in theology, and whether they had appeared in a previous Passion. That Bach changed texts at all is not the only evidence that points to his concern for textual fit and propriety. So, too, do his varied and nuanced methods for treating existing texts, which range from minimal tweaking of an existing text, to substantial revisions, to redrafting a poem,

---

11. In Table 2.3 (as in Table 2.2), movements given the same number in CPEB:CW and BR-CPEB are typically counted as one interpolation unless these fall into different categories. The borrowings in the category "Other" come from the Graun brothers and from C. P. E. Bach's Magnificat (Wq 215) and his Litanies (Wq 204).

12. As noted earlier, chorales and song arrangements are excluded from this discussion.

Table 2.3. Origin of borrowed movements in C. P. E. Bach's Passions
(excluding narratives, chorales, and song arrangements)

	J. S. Bach	Stölzel	Homilius	Benda	Installation Cantatas	Other
1769	1					1
1770			6			
1771		4	2	2		
1772	1	4	2			
1773			10			
1774			9			
1775			7			
1776			6			
1777			1	2	3	1
1778			7	1		
1779		1*	1	1	4	
1780			2	3		1
1781			1*	2	1	
1782				2		
1783				1		
1784				2		
1785						1
1786						
1787						
1788						
1789			6*			1

Note: An asterisk indicates that one or more movements are a secondary borrowing; the more immediate model is in one of Bach's Passions.

to substituting a new, alternate text for an original from a model movement. Studying these procedures for their own sake not only enlightens us as to Bach's working method as a composer who dealt regularly with texts but also provides analogues for his approaches to musical revision, some of which will be explored below.

On one end of the spectrum of textual revision in Bach's Passions lie those borrowed movements that exhibit only minor changes or none at all. Most examples of this sort originated in Passions (or occasionally in cantatas) with texts that could be slipped into the same or similar positions in Bach's liturgical Passions because they were already appropriate for the occasion. Their poetic language also needed no updating, nor did their theological messages or emphases. The majority of such model movements come from the several Passions and cantatas by Homilius and the one Passion by Stölzel (see "Borrowed from Other Composers" in Table 2.1). Essentially, these were good enough to leave alone.

However, some texts underwent more significant revision. A well-known example of this can be found in Bach's first *St. John Passion* (H 785), performed for Hamburg congregations in 1772. The penultimate movement for this work, the chorus "Ruht wohl, ihr heiligen Gebeine," stems from the movement of the same title in his father's own setting of this same Evangelist (BWV 245, no. 67), itself featuring a text derived, in part, from the penultimate movement (the aria "Wisch ab der Tränen scharfe Lauge") in the Passion poem by Barthold Heinrich Brockes, a work beloved by poets and composers of Johann Sebastian's generation.[13] As Philipp Emanuel fashioned his Passion for 1772, he emended the poetry from his father's chorus directly in the BWV 245 performing materials themselves, crossing out portions of the original text in the alto concertante part and jotting his own version in ink underneath (see Figure 2.1). Rather than a minor tweaking of the original poem, the younger Bach's revision presents a major alteration that still echoes the original (see Table 2.4).[14] The radical departure occurs after the first two lines, with the third and subsequent lines taking occasional word cues from the model but offering a linguistic modernization of the original poem's more old-fashioned formulations. The version penned by the Hamburg Bach also shifts the theological perspective toward one that is more personal and positive in its formulation.

Further instances of this variety of substantial textual revision exist beyond the 1772 example, but they present such radical reworkings that one could even consider them new poems, heavily inspired by the original. One such poem was based on the text of the aria "Vor Dir, dem Vater, der verzeiht" from Homilius's *St. John Passion* (HoWV I.4, no. 16), first used by Bach in his 1774 Passion (H 787, no. 15).[15] When

13. Barthold Heinrich Brockes, *Der für die Sünde der Welt gemarterte und sterbende Jesus aus den IV Evangelisten. In gebundener Rede vorgestellt und in der Fasten-Zeit Musicalisch auffgeführet* (Hamburg: Conrad Neumann, 1715).

14. Text and translation of BWV 245, no. 67, in Table 2.4 from Alfred Dürr, *Johann Sebastian Bach's "St. John Passion": Genesis, Transmission and Meaning*, trans. Alfred Clayton (Oxford: Oxford University Press, 2000); originally published as *Die Johannes-Passion von Johann Sebastian Bach. Entstehung, Überlieferung, Werkeinführung* (Kassel: Bärenreiter, 1988), 168–71, 176–77. Dürr's suggestion that the new text version written in place of the original might belong to a planned fourth version by Johann Sebastian can be corrected with this new information. Arthur Mendel had already noted the concordance between the alternate text in D-B, Mus. ms. Bach St 111, and the textbook from C. P. E. Bach's *St. John Passion* of 1772, as mentioned in Stephen Lewis Clark, "The Occasional Choral Works of C. P. E. Bach" (Ph.D. diss., Princeton University, 1984), 111.

15. Additional and even more extreme instances of this procedure can be seen in the text for Bach's aria "Erfrecht euch nur, die Unschuld zu verklagen" from the 1789 Passion (no. 19), based on Homilius's aria "Verdammt ihn nur, ihr ungerechten Richter" from his *St. Mark Passion* (HoWV I.10, no. 23), as well as for the text of "Versammelt euch, der Erde gefallne Kinder" from the 1781 Passion (no. 26),

Table 2.4. "Ruht wohl, ihr heiligen Gebeine" in J. S. Bach, *St. John Passion* (BWV 245), no. 67, and in C. P. E. Bach, *St. John Passion* (1772), no. 23

J. S. Bach, BWV 245, no. 67	*C. P. E. Bach, 1772 Passion, no. 23*
Ruht wohl, ihr heiligen Gebeine,	**Ruht wohl, ihr heiligen Gebeine,**
die ich nun **weiter nicht beweine,**	Um **die ich nicht mehr** trostlos **weine:**
ruht wohl und **bringt** auch **mich** zur **Ruh.**	Ich weiß, einst **giebt** der Tod **mir Ruh.**
Das **Grab,** so euch bestimmet ist,	Nicht stets umschliesset mich die **Gruft;**
und ferner keine Not umschließt,	Einst, wenn Gott, mein Erlöser, ruft,
macht mir den **Himmel** auf und schließt die	Dann eil' auch ich verklärt dem **Himmel**
Hölle **zu.**	Gottes **zu.**
Sleep well, ye holy relics,	*Sleep well, ye holy relics,*
Which I no longer now bewail,	*For which disconsolate I weep no more,*
Sleep well and also bring me to sleep!	*I know that death will give me sleep.*
The grave, which is your destined place	*Not always shall the grave surround me,*
And now no sorrow knows,	*And once, when God, my Savior, calls,*
Doth open heaven up for me and shuts the gates	*Then to God's heaven I speed transfigured.*
of hell.	

Figure 2.1. Leipzig alto concertante part from J. S. Bach's *St. John Passion* (BWV 245), showing original text underlay for "Ruht wohl, ihr heiligen Gebeine" replaced with parody text in C. P. E. Bach's hand (D-B, Mus. ms. Bach St 111, fascicle II, p. 354). Reproduced with permission.

Bach once again borrowed this movement for his 1789 Passion (H 802, no. 14), he reworked the text so that it retains the same basic message and even many of the same words (see Table 2.5).[16]

On the most extreme end of textual changes lies the substitution of an entirely new text for the original, a so-called parody text. Bach used this procedure most often for movements that he pulled from works other than Passions, including occasional cantatas and liturgical cantatas that fell outside of the Lenten season. Parody texts were also employed for movements that were derived from Passions of other composers but that did not fit the position in the narrative of the new work, as well as for movements that he had previously used in one of his own Passions. Two-thirds of the movements with origins in Benda's cantatas were furnished with new texts, as were many of those from Bach's own pastoral installation cantatas and, obviously, the two Italian-language arias by the Graun brothers (see "Borrowed from Other Composers" and "Self-Borrowed" in Table 2.1).

One of the most illustrative examples of parody procedure in Bach's Passions comes not from the typical sources of Benda and the pastoral installation cantatas but rather

Table 2.5. Text of Homilius, "Vor Dir, dem Vater, der verzeiht" (1774 Passion, no. 15), and parody text, "Im Staub gebückt" (1789 Passion, no. 14)

Homilius, HoWV I.4, no. 16; Bach, 1774 Passion, no. 15	Bach, 1789 Passion, no. 14
Vor Dir, dem **Vater**, der verzeiht, **Bewein' ich** meinen Fall voll Reue. Ach **Vater** der **Barmherzigkeit**, Gott, sey mir **gnädig**, und **verzeihe**!	Im Staub gebückt **wein' ich vor dir**, O **Vater**, über meine Sünden. **Barmherziger! verzeihe** mir, Und laß mich **Gnade** vor dir finden.
Before you, the father who forgives, *I bewail my fall, full of remorse.* *Oh, father of mercy,* *God, be merciful to me, and forgive!*	*I cry before you, stooping in the dust,* *Oh father, on account of my sins.* *Merciful one! Forgive me,* *And let me find mercy before you.*

which appears to be based in part on the text for the opening movement for Bach's *Musik am Dankfeste wegen des fertigen Michaelisturms* (H 823), titled "Versammlet euch dem Herrn zu Ehren." See Moira Leanne Hill, "Carl Philipp Emanuel Bach's Passion Settings: Context, Content, and Impact" (Ph.D. diss., Yale University, 2015), 259, 264.

16. German text in Table 2.5 is published in CPEB:CW, VIII/3.1: *Librettos I (Passions)*, ed. Ulrich Leisinger (Los Altos, Calif.: Packard Humanities Institute, 2011), 90, 329. These and all subsequent English translations by the author. Throughout this essay, tables and passages that contain a work's poetic text retain the orthography of the original printed libretto, when available.

from a rare instance in which Bach parodies a Homilius aria: it shows this procedure used first for narrative fit and then again when the movement is reused in a later Passion. The original aria, "Mensch, empfinde doch Erbarmen," taken from Homilius's *St. Mark Passion* (HoWV I.10, no. 3), references Jesus teaching his disciples about helping those less fortunate (see Table 2.6).[17] Bach placed this movement in his 1772 *St. John Passion* (no. 15), where it appears immediately after Pilate leads Jesus, crowned with thorns, out before the crowd that had gathered. The parody text selected by Bach, "So freiwillig, ohne Klage," suits this position well, even echoing Pilate's mocking pronouncement "Behold the man!" When the composer reused this aria in his 1780 *St. John Passion* (H 793, no. 17), he kept it in the same narrative position but gave it a new text, as he typically did when a musical setting appeared in more than one Passion. In fact, the two instances that break this rule both come from Bach's final Passion, the St. Matthew setting of 1789, which he compiled at the very end of his life.[18]

In much the same way that he had altered his father's performing materials for the *St. John Passion* when revising the text of the chorus "Ruht wohl, ihr heiligen Gebeine," Bach used his physical copy of the model for his aria "So freiwillig, ohne Klage" from the 1772 Passion as a medium in which to record his parody text. In this latter case, he entered the alternate text into the empty staff beneath the borrowed movement in the autograph score for Homilius's *St. Mark Passion* from his personal library (D-B, SA 37; see Figure 2.2).

The above examples have shown how Bach treated the texts of arias, *accompagnati*, choruses, and similar movements that he borrowed for use in his liturgical Passions. Beyond deciding whether to alter these texts at all, Bach arrived at creative and sensitive methods for obtaining appropriate poetry, ranging from minor modifications, to more thorough revisions that retain aspects of the model poem, to discarding the old text for an entirely new one. What spurred these changes could differ as well. At times he seemed motivated by a desire to improve outdated aspects of the model poems, and at other times he elected to use a poem that better fit the necessary narrative position or that even offered a new text when a musical setting was reused in a later Passion. And because the different categories of models that he worked with fulfilled his needs to varying degrees, some required more attention than others.

17. Homilius's text in Table 2.6 is found in D-B, SA 37, 18v–24r; Bach's two texts are published in CPEB:CW, VIII/3.1, 58, 186–87.

18. These two cases are the accompaniment "Die Feinde rüsten sich" from the 1789 Passion (no. 18), which he had previously inserted into his 1773 Passion (H 786, no. 7), and the aria "Verachtete, verdammte Sünder," which appeared as no. 25 in the 1789 Passion and which he had also used in 1773 (no. 8). Both come from Homilius's Passion oratorio *Nun, ihr, meiner Augen Lider* (HoWV I.9, nos. 6 and 7 respectively). For the 1789 Passion, see CPEB:CW, IV/4.6 (forthcoming).

Table 2.6. Text of Homilius, "Mensch, empfinde doch Erbarmen" (HoWV I.10, no. 3), and parody texts, "So freiwillig, ohne Klage" (1772 Passion, no. 15) and "Um in Schwachheit mich zu stärken" (1780 Passion, no. 17)

Homilius, HoWV I.10, no. 3	Bach, 1772 Passion, no. 15	Bach, 1780 Passion, no. 17
Mensch, empfinde doch Erbarmen,	So freywillig, ohne Klage	Um in Schwachheit mich zu stärken,
Brich dem Hungrigen dein Brot,	Trägt der Heilige die Schmach;	Wirst du, Heiland, selbst jetzt schwach.
Kleide die entblößten Armen,	Dessen Blick am bessern Tage	Tief in denen blutgen Wunden,
Weine mit in ihre Noth!	Weinend über Salem brach!	Daraus mir ein Balsam quillt.
Wenn dein Bruder ängstlich klaget	Selbst der Richter fühlt die Grösse	Hab ich neue Kraft empfunden,
Sieh ihn dann mit Mitleid an!	Dieses stillen Vorwurfs schwer;	Die des Zweifels Ohnmacht stillt.
Weißt du, was dein Richter saget:	Fühlet eigne Scham und Blöße;	Laß mich, kömmt mein Sterbetag,
Dies, dies habt ihr mir gethan.	Ruft: O, welch ein Mensch ist Er!	Trostvoll ihre Wirkung fühlen!
Man, feel mercy,	*Thus, voluntarily, without complaint*	*To strengthen me in my weakness,*
Break your bread with the hungry,	*Does the holy one bear dishonor;*	*You yourself, redeemer, have now become weak.*
Clothe the naked poor,	*Whose gaze on a better day*	*Deep from within your bloody wounds*
Cry along in their hour of need!	*Burst out crying over Jerusalem!*	*Springs a balsam for me.*
When your brother wails with fear,	*Even the judge himself feels the magnitude*	*I have felt new strength*
Regard him then with compassion!	*Of this silent accusation with heaviness;*	*That calms the powerlessness of doubt.*
You know what your judge says:	*He feels his own shame and nakedness;*	*When the day of my death arrives, let me,*
You have done this unto me.	*He calls out: Oh, behold the man!*	*Filled with comfort, feel your impact!*

Figure 2.2. Homilius, "Mensch, empfinde doch Erbarmen" (HoWV I.10, no. 3; autograph score), with parody text and other entries written by C. P. E. Bach (D-B, SA 37, fol. 22r). Reproduced with permission.

Bach's drive to modify did not confine itself to the texts. In the musical settings of these borrowed interpolations in his Passions, not only did he adjust the music of his models to align with his own taste and goals—just as he did with the poetry—but his methods in doing so were also varied and nuanced.

Changes to the Music

The methods by which Bach altered the musical settings that he borrowed for interpolated movements in his Passions vary considerably, as does the degree to which he applied these methods to his models. As with the texts, clear motivations can be discerned for his musical revisions. An entire category of changes can be traced back to practical concerns that included how many musicians were at Bach's disposal during any given year and their differing abilities. These modifications include things such as transpositions and changes to the scoring that affect the orchestration, and delegation of voice parts. Adjustments of that sort will not be explored in this study; rather, this essay will focus on those changes connected with Bach's emendations to the text and those explained neither by practical considerations nor by textual parody and revision.[19]

Bach's revision of the music of these borrowed movements ranges from little or none, to updating the melodies alone, to rewriting whole passages, to something approaching a true recomposition of a model. Deleting entire formal sections was another tool that he used to modify borrowings that featured ternary form (that is, da capo or ABA structure, along with its variants). The reasons behind the use of these various tools of revision also differed. Some relate to the substitution of a new text for the old one; others appear to be purely a matter of aesthetic preference. The manner in which a new

19. For a consideration of how these factors affected Bach's compositional and compilational choices, see Hill, "Carl Philipp Emanuel Bach's Passion Settings," 22–113.

text was set to existing music brings its own assortment of aesthetic considerations as well, and at times these parody texts are accommodated with alterations to the music.

Clear trends emerge in how and when these procedures for altering borrowed material were applied. First, they tend to correlate to where the model came from. For instance, Bach often revised Benda's melodies but less frequently revised those of Homilius and Stölzel. Second, the use of these procedures shifts over time. For example, as the years progressed, Bach moved away from the aesthetic of the da capo aria toward a preference for through-composed music by increasingly eliminating the return to the A section, and sometimes omitting the B section as well.

Closely related to the changes made to the music is the way that Bach fit his parody texts to his models. This could affect such aspects as how much text was presented in a given amount of music, as well as how much text repetition occurred and whether this included single words, phrases, or whole lines of poetry. It also affected the degree to which the settings were syllabic or melismatic.

These general observations on Bach's process of adapting music for a new purpose are well illustrated using several concrete musical examples. In the discussion below, these are arranged in four groups; each centers on one of four models together with its various appearances in the Passions: (1) an aria by Stölzel that Bach used first with its original text in 1772 and again parodied in 1779; (2) an aria by Homilius that appeared in the Passions of 1772 and 1780, parodied both times; (3) an aria by Benda parodied for use in 1784; and (4) a parodied version of a Homilius aria from Bach's last Passion (1789).

GROUP I

An early example of Bach's musical reworking of a model can be found in the *St. John Passion* of 1772. This larger work, like the St. Luke setting of the previous year, incorporated four borrowings from Stölzel's Passion oratorio *Sechs geistliche Betrachtungen* (1741). The movements adopted from this source were largely left in their original state, with two exceptions: Bach parodied one duet and significantly revised the musical setting of one aria at several points. The aria, "Liebste Hand! ich küsse dich" (no. 5 in the 1772 Passion), exhibits musical revisions that range from slight to consequential. In sum, approximately fourteen measures scattered throughout the work were added or rewritten by Bach, not counting the various smaller alterations that he introduced as well.[20] A representative sample of these is encapsulated in the passage that spans the musical phrase starting at the first vocal entry (see Examples 2.1a and 2.1b).[21] In

20. One silent and purely notational change affects the time signature of this aria, which Bach adjusted to 3/4 from Stölzel's 3/8.

21. The excerpt from Stölzel's aria in Example 1a is found in D-B, Mus. ms. 21401, fol. 15v–15r. The excerpt of Bach's 1772 Passion (no. 5) in Example 2.1b is from CPEB:CW, IV/7.1: *Passion According to*

Example 2.1a. G. H. Stölzel, "Liebste Hand! ich küsse dich"
(*Sechs geistliche Betrachtungen*, 1741).

Example 2.1b. Bach, "Liebste Hand! ich küsse dich" (1772 Passion, no. 5).

Bach's version, the alto part's opening motive, a descending leap of a fifth, was filled in for greater stepwise melodic motion, as was a small leap in the following measure on the word "küsse." These changes are dwarfed in scope by his extension of the cadence that ends this larger musical phrase, which drastically lengthened Stölzel's pedal point on the dominant and introduced chromaticism to the vocal line. As these more radical revisions have no obvious practical benefit to the singers, nor do they relate in any way to changes affecting the text (there were none here), the decision to undertake them appears to be aesthetic in nature, done for the purpose of "improving" the musical substance.

Seven years after Bach first incorporated this aria into a Passion, he did so yet again. This time he took as a starting point his own reworked version from 1772, furnished it with a new text, and made additional changes to the music, resulting in the aria "Ach, dass wir Erbarmung fünden" from the 1779 *St. Luke Passion* (no. 4). The old and new texts are roughly comparable in length, differing only by one line, but they diverge in line length and in whether lines begin with a stressed or an unstressed syllable (see Table 2.7).[22] Naturally, Bach had complete freedom to determine the underlay of the parody text, including choices such as where syllables fell within the melody, the repetition of words or phrases, and the order in which the poem's lines were presented. The new text that Bach selected actually has one fewer line than the old one, but the composer also chose to excise the entire B section of the aria. This meant that all six lines of the new text were set to the music of the A section, instead of just three lines in the original version (see Table 2.8).[23] Originally, Stölzel had set lines 1, 2, and 3 in the A section (twice, in consecutive order, surrounded by instrumental ritornelli), and lines 4 through 7 in the B section, with some repetition. For Bach's version from 1779, compressing six lines of parody text into a space for three resulted in less text repetition, by virtue of having more text appear in the same amount of melodic material.

Table 2.7. Text of Stölzel, "Liebste Hand! ich küsse dich" (1772 Passion, no. 5), and parody text, "Ach, dass wir Erbarmung fünden" (1779 Passion, no. 4)

Bach, 1772 Passion, no. 5	*Bach, 1779 Passion, no. 4*
1 Liebste Hand! ich küsse dich,	1 Ach, daß wir Erbarmung fünden
2 Denn Du lässest auch für mich	2 Trugst du unsre Sünden!
3 Dich mit Banden hart belegen.	3 Gott nahm sie von uns, und warf sie auf dich.
4 Ewiglich gehört auch ich,	4 Wir giengen in der Irre, wie Schafe:
5 Meiner Missethaten wegen,	5 Auf dir lag unsre Strafe;
6 In der Hölle Folterhaus:	6 An dir rächte Gott sich.
7 Doch Du ziehest mich heraus.	
Dearest hand! I kiss you,	*Oh, so that we might obtain mercy*
For you allow yourself	*You bore our sins!*
To be bound tightly with ties for me.	*God took them from us, and cast them upon you.*
* For an eternity I, too, belonged*	*We have gone astray, like sheep:*
* In the torture chamber of Hell*	*Our punishment lay on you;*
* Because of my misdeeds,*	*God avenged himself on you.*
* But you pull me out from there.*	

St. John (1772), ed. Paul Corneilson (Los Altos, Calif.: Packard Humanities Institute, 2007), 11–12; 128–31 (appendix) includes a full transcription of the model from Stölzel.

22. The texts in Table 2.7 are published in CPEB:CW, VIII/3.1, 53, 164.

23. The works compared in Table 2.8 are published in CPEB:CW, IV/7.1 (1772 Passion); and CPEB:CW, IV/6.3: *Passion According to St. Luke (1779)*, ed. Ellen Exner (Los Altos, Calif.: Packard Humanities Institute, 2016).

Table 2.8. Text setting and aria structures for Stölzel, "Liebste Hand! ich küsse dich" (1772 Passion, no. 5), and its parody, "Ach, dass wir Erbarmung fünden" (1779 Passion, no. 4)

1772 Passion, no. 5	*1779 Passion, no. 4*
A section	**A section**
Rit. 1 2 3 Rit. 1 2 3 Rit.	Rit. 1 2 3 Rit. 4 5 6 5 6 Rit.
B section	[B section omitted]
4 5 6 4 5 6 7 7 7 7	
da capo	

Compared to Bach's version of this Stölzel aria from the 1772 Passion, his version from 1779 features other changes as well (see Example 2.2).[24] Again taking the opening phrase of the vocal line as a representative example, one immediately observes that the first several measures of the melody are simplified. In addition, Bach effectively shortened the melisma by adding more text to the first measure and a half, thus making the text setting of this portion syllabic. The portion of the melisma that was retained now corresponds with a word—"warf" ("cast" or "threw")—that contains the appropriate emotional charge, just as in the model where this melodic element had lined up with the verb "belegen" ("to bind"). Needless to say, which word a melisma emphasized was another consideration that a composer setting a parody text to music needed to take into account.

GROUP 2

Another set of examples that reveals Bach's reshaping of borrowed musical material involves the aria "Mensch, empfinde doch Erbarmen," from Homilius's *St. Mark Passion*. As discussed earlier, Bach first used this movement in his 1772 Passion with a parody text and then revised it again in 1780, setting its music to yet a different poem. In his many borrowings from Homilius's Passions and cantatas, Bach tended to preserve most of the original musical material, especially when keeping the model's poem intact. This aria in its parodied form from 1772 largely follows this trend, though a somewhat higher proportion of the tenor part's vocal line (about a third) was tweaked or rewritten; the instrumental lines were preserved in their original form with only minor exceptions. As seen in Figure 2.2, Bach's melodic revisions were sparse enough that he could enter them alongside the parody text into empty staves in the autograph score of Homilius's work from his personal library. The 1780 version does not stray

24. The excerpts in Example 2.2 are from CPEB:CW, IV/7.1, 11–12 (1772 Passion); and CPEB:CW, IV/6.3, 26–30 (1779 Passion).

Example 2.2. "Liebste Hand! ich küsse dich" (1772 Passion, no. 5) and parody,
"Ach, daß wir Erbarmung fünden" (1779 Passion, no. 4).

far from either the 1772 version or the original by Homilius. It even exhibits readings
from both, suggesting that in 1780 Bach referenced both the original model and his
first revision, probably in the autograph score that he had marked up for 1772. This
fact muddies the distinction that is often made between primary and secondary borrowings, as this aria exhibits characteristics of each category.

The three versions of this aria are generally quite similar. Excerpts of the same passage from the model by Homilius, from Bach's 1772 version, and from his 1780 version
showing the final portion of the vocal part that appears before the closing ritornello
illustrate this point (see Example 2.3).[25] In this passage, and in the aria more gener-

25. The excerpts in Example 2.3 are from Gottfried August Homilius, *Markuspassion: HoWV I.10*,
ed. Uwe Wolf (Stuttgart: Carus-Verlag, 2011), 20–27; CPEB:CW, IV/7.1, 54–62 (1772 Passion); and

Example 2.3. Homilius, "Mensch, empfinde doch Erbarmen" (HoWV I.10, no. 3),
and parody versions, "So freiwillig, ohne Klage" (1772 Passion, no. 15)
and "Um in Schwachheit mich zu stärken" (1780 Passion, no. 17).

ally, the version from 1780 deviates in one important respect: its text setting. Focusing merely on this excerpt, one notices that in this late version Bach set syllabically a portion that had been a melisma on the words "weine" or "weinend" (mm. 101–6), just as he had shortened the melisma in the example from a 1779 parody of a Stölzel aria discussed above. Next, Bach advances to a new line of text in the 1780 version (m. 107), whereas in his 1772 version of this aria, a phrase that had already appeared was simply repeated as in the model. In fact, Bach omitted the entire B section of this aria in 1780, but he selected a replacement text of the same length as in both his 1772 version and in the original by Homilius (see Table 2.9).[26] As a consequence, in 1780 he accommodated eight lines of text with the same amount of music that had previously featured just four. He decreased the amount of text repetition as a result of this choice, much as he had in the previous set of examples based on the Stölzel aria.

GROUP 3

Bach's Passions from 1777 through 1784 each include from one to three movements taken from a cycle of cantatas by Benda, setting texts from a collection by the contemporary poet Balthasar Münter. A further example illustrating how Bach altered the musical substance of his borrowings comes from this so-called Münter cycle. Bach's aria "Die Unschuld wird verfolgt," appearing in his 1784 Passion, was parodied from Benda's cantata *Ihr brausenden Wogen, bestürmet die Lüfte* (L 518) from this collection.[27] Not only does it encompass changes to the model's ABA structure of the sort already referenced, but it also exemplifies a new type of alteration not yet discussed: extreme and comprehensive melodic revision. This phenomenon appears to be related, in part, to the greater use of parody texts for his borrowings from Benda; two-thirds of these received a different text from their original, a proportion much higher than that for the borrowings from Stölzel and Homilius. The melodies of the movements by Benda that Bach took for his Passions but did not parody remained largely untouched, but when he did provide an alternate text, he typically introduced changes to the vocal part. These could range from conservative adjustments to virtual recomposition. "Die Unschuld wird verfolgt" is representative of the extreme end of melodic revision

---

CPEB:CW, IV/7.3, *Passion According to St. John (1780)*, ed. Paul Corneilson (Los Altos, Calif.: Packard Humanities Institute, 2017), 53–62. A transcription of the original aria by Homilius is published in CPEB:CW, IV/7.1, 132–35 (appendix).

26. For translation of Table 2.9 text, see Table 2.6.

27. The identity of this model was uncovered by Jason B. Grant and first published in his essay "A Borrowing Identified in Carl Philipp Emanuel Bach's 1784 St. John Passion and a Sketch Explained," in *The Sons of Bach: Essays for Elias N. Kulukundis*, ed. Peter Wollny and Stephen Roe (Ann Arbor: Steglein, 2016), 47–55.

Table 2.9. Text and structure for Homilius, "Mensch, empfinde doch Erbarmen" (HoWV I.10, no. 3), and for Bach's two parody versions (1772 Passion, no. 15, and 1780 Passion, no. 17)

Homilius, HoWV I.10, no. 3	*Bach, 1772 Passion, no. 15*	*Bach, 1780 Passion, no. 17*
1 Mensch, empfinde doch Erbarmen,	1 So freywillig, ohne Klage	1 Um in Schwachheit mich zu stärken,
2 Brich dem Hungrigen dein Brot,	2 Trägt der Heilige die Schmach;	2 Wirst du, Heiland, selbst jetzt schwach.
3 Kleide die entblößten Armen,	3 Dessen Blick am bessern Tage	3 Tief in denen blutgen Wunden,
4 Weine mit in ihre Noth!	4 Weinend über Salem brach!	4 Daraus mir ein Balsam quillt.
5 Wenn dein Bruder ängstlich klaget	5 Selbst der Richter fühlt die Grösse	5 Hab ich neue Kraft empfunden,
6 Sieh ihn dann mit Mitleid an!	6 Dieses stillen Vorwurfs schwer;	6 Die des Zweifels Ohnmacht stillt.
7 Weißt du, was dein Richter saget:	7 Fühlet eigne Scham und Blöße;	7 Laß mich, kömmt mein Sterbetag,
8 Dies, habt ihr mir gethan.	8 Ruft: O, welch ein Mensch ist Er!	8 Trostvoll ihre Wirkung fühlen!
A section	**A section**	**A section**
Rit. 1 2 3 4	Rit. 1 2 3 4	Rit. 1 2 3 4 5 6
Rit. 1 2 3 4 2 1 3 4 Rit.	Rit. 1 2 3 4 2 1 3 4 Rit.	Rit. 7 8 3 5 6 1 2 (2, partial) 7 8 Rit.
B section	**B section**	
5 6 6 7 8 (7, partial) 8 Rit.	5 6 7 5 8 5/8 8 Rit.	[B section omitted]
dal segno	dal segno	

Figure 2.3. C. P. E. Bach, sketch of parody aria "Die Unschuld wird verfolgt,"
for 1784 Passion, no. 12 (D-LEb, Kulukundis I.3–4). Reproduced with permission.

observed in this category of models, to the point that Bach found it useful to sketch
his vocal melody out in advance, including key syllables and words from his chosen
poem to indicate the text's alignment (see Figure 2.3).

The parody text that Bach selected for Benda's model "Droht nur, ihr Gefahren" is
roughly the same length as the original, when one takes into account the omission of
both the B section and the da capo return in the 1784 version (see Table 2.10).[28] The
number of syllables per line sometimes exceeds the original, but not by very much.
Some adjustment of the melody was required to accommodate this new text, but the
changes that Bach introduced to the vocal line exceeded what was necessary.

A closer examination of the vocal part of this aria reveals Bach's approach. Benda's
version can be characterized as featuring short bursts of melodic activity punctuated
by rests (see Example 2.4).[29] Bach links these up. He also regularizes the rhythm of the

28. Benda's text in Table 2.10 is found in D-B, Mus. ms. 1334, fascicle IV, fol. 41v-44r; Bach's text is
published in CPEB:CW, VIII/3.1, 249.

29. The Benda model and Bach's sketch have been transposed to aid comparison with the version
from Bach's 1784 Passion. The excerpt of Benda's cantata in Example 2.4 is from D-B, Mus. ms.
1334, fascicle IV, fol. 41v-44r; Bach sketch is from D-LEb, Kulukundis I.3–4; and Bach's 1784 version is from CPEB:CW, IV/7.4, *Passion According to St. John (1784)*, ed. Paul Corneilson (Los Altos,

Table 2.10. Text of Benda, "Droht nur, ihr Gefahren" (*Ihr brausenden Wogen,*
bestürmet die Lüfte, L 518), and parody text, "Die Unschuld wird verfolgt"
(1784 Passion, no. 12)

Benda, L 518	Bach, 1784 Passion, no. 12
Droht nur ihr Gefahren,	Die Unschuld wird verfolgt!
Muthig steh ich da.	Die kühnsten Bösewichter
Kommt in wilden Schaaren	Ziehn trotzig wider sie in Streit.
Auf mich hergefahren,	Sie fleht, und findet hier
Gott wird mich bewahren,	Nicht einen güt'gen Richter,
Denn er ist mir nah.	Der ihr die Hand zum Schutze beut.
Dir will ich vertrauen	
In der bösen Zeit;	[B section omitted]
Laß dein Antlitz schauen,	
Gott voll Gütigkeit.	
Just you threaten, you dangers,	*Innocence is being persecuted!*
I stand courageously.	*The bold evildoers*
When the wild droves	*Battle defiantly against it.*
Approach me,	*It pleads but finds here*
God will save me,	*Not even one benevolent judge*
For he is near to me.	*Who offers it a protective hand.*
I want to trust you	
In the time of evil;	
Let your countenance look upon me,	
God, full of benevolence.	

opening measure (m. 13)—a change that was not strictly needed, although the addition of an upbeat (d') on beat 4 of measure 14 and the deletion of the same pitch from beat 2 were necessary to ensure that the melodic stresses corresponded with accented syllables in the text. Starting at the second line of text (m. 15), Bach simplifies the model's melodic gesture and smooths out the rhythm of Benda's model, then follows immediately with the third line of text instead of pausing as Benda had done. From there, Bach's version continues to diverge from his model, often by reducing the number of melodic leaps (for example, mm. 21 and 25). In its text setting, Bach's version, like Benda's, is syllabic but contains less repetition of small phrases and word pairs than in the model.

Calif.: Packard Humanities Institute, 2018), 34–37. A full transcription of Bach's sketch is published in CPEB:CW, IV/7.4, 104–5; whereas that transcription editorially completes the sketch's fragmentary text, the transcription in Example 2.4 preserves this aspect of Bach's rough draft to illustrate his working process.

Example 2.4. Benda, "Droht nur, ihr Gefahren" (L 518), with C. P. E. Bach's
sketch (D-LEb, Kulukundis I.3–4) and parody version, "Die Unschuld
wird verfolgt" (1784 Passion, no. 12).

Example 2.4. Continued.

GROUP 4

The final example of musical revision comes from Bach's final Passion, the setting of St. Matthew that was performed in 1789, the year after his death. As noted earlier, this work deviated from the trend toward greater inclusion of original material that is observed in Bach's works from the 1780s, culminating in the *St. John Passion* of 1788, where borrowing occurs only in the narrative and chorales. In contrast to that Passion, Bach composed only one movement for his last Passion. Six of the remaining non-chorale interpolations (that is, five arias and one *accompagnato*) are derived from Homilius. Of the five arias, four are both parodied and drastically revised in a manner unlike anything Bach had done before in this genre. His reworkings involved excising numerous smaller and larger segments of music and recomposing the transitions between the remaining passages.

The last of these four parodied and revised arias, "Erfrecht euch nur, die Unschuld zu verklagen" (1789 Passion, no. 19), allows for a detailed examination of the processes of parody and revision, since this movement is associated with an extant autograph sketch that contains a draft version of much of its vocal part, like the Benda example studied above (see Figure 2.4). Unlike the Benda example, however, here Bach made relatively few changes to the parts of the melody that he retained, so the sketch appears to have helped him keep track of the extensive deletions and rewritings that he carried out on Homilius's aria, as well as his decisions for text underlay.

Yet another parallel can be drawn between Bach's "Erfrecht euch nur" and a different example studied above. Although Bach had first borrowed and revised the model "Verdammt ihn nur" from Homilius's *St. Mark Passion* (HoWV I.10, no. 23) for an interpolation in his 1770 Passion (no. 13), for the more heavily reworked version in his 1789 Passion he returned to the readings from the original version by Homilius.[30] This is similar to the case in which Bach borrowed Homilius's aria "Mensch, empfinde doch Erbarmen" for an interpolation for his 1772 Passion (no. 15), and then revisited Homilius's version when crafting "Um in Schwachheit mich zu stärken" for 1780 (no. 17)—though in this instance he also took readings from his own earlier version. However, the mixture of readings in the 1780 Passion has no practical explanation and appears to reflect Bach's aesthetic preferences, whereas the few alterations that he made to Homilius's "Verdammt ihn nur" for 1770 effectively lowered the vocal range to align more closely with his tenor's capabilities. Apparently these were not necessary for 1789, as he had designated the vocal part to be sung by a soprano and could thus revert to Homilius's original readings.[31]

---

30. Scores for these works are published in Homilius, *Markuspassion*, 61–67 (HoWV I.10); CPEB:CW, IV/5.1, *Passion According to St. Mark (1770)*, ed. Uwe Wolf (Los Altos, Calif.: Packard Humanities Institute, 2006), 26–40; and CPEB:CW, IV/4.6 (1789 Passion; forthcoming).

31. Notably, both variants would have been visible to him while he was working from the autograph

Figure 2.4. C. P. E. Bach, sketch of parody aria "Erfrecht euch nur, die Unschuld zu verklagen," for 1789 Passion, no. 19 (D-B, SA 5136, fol. 28v). Reproduced with permission.

Bach's revisions included removing portions ranging in size from one to sixteen measures, scattered throughout the work. His larger deletions trimmed down ritornelli to a third or even a quarter of their original size. He also removed the second part from each half of the A section as well as the final third of the B section. To ensure continuity, he rewrote transitions at three places, each about six measures in length. Although Bach's version features a da capo return to the A section like Homilius's original, it presents its musical material far more succinctly. These excisions also had the effect of removing several major melismas. The one melisma that Bach decided to keep was considerably shortened and simplified through recomposition (see Examples 2.5 and 2.6).[32]

Bach's method of text setting in "Erfrecht euch nur" differed greatly from that of the original Homilius aria. Even though his chosen parody text was one line shorter than

_____

score of Homilius's Passion in his possession (D-B, SA 37), as he had entered the variants for 1770 into this source. See, for example, his emendations to the vocal part visible on fols. 49v–52v of SA 37.

32. Example 2.5 is excerpted from Homilius, *Markuspassion*, 61–67. Bach's aria in Example 2.6 is in CPEB:CW, IV/4.6.

Example 2.5. Homilius, "Verdammt ihn nur, ihr ungerechten Richter"
(HoWV I.10, no. 23), mm. 31–49.

the model's, Bach significantly shortened the model musically, which again leads to a reduction in text repetition (see Table 2.11).[33] Furthermore, the specific way that Bach shortened his model through excision avoids the repetition of single words and short phrases found in Homilius's version. An example of this occurs in the corresponding excerpts presented in Examples 2.5 and 2.6, where a short musical and textual echo is removed ("den Schöpfer der Natur" versus "des grossen Schöpfers Hohn"). The repetition of single words and short phrases could seem stylized and artificial. Instead, Bach avoided this and mostly cycled through the lines of text sequentially before repeating larger sections. This approach is particularly evident in the comparative charts of text repetition for the model and for Bach's version shown in Table 2.12.[34]

33. Homilius's text in Table 2.11 is published in *Markuspassion*, 61–67; Bach's text is in CPEB:CW, VIII/3.1, 331.

34. Scores used for Table 2.12 are in D-B, SA 37, 18v-24r (Homilius); CPEB:CW, IV/5.1 (1770 Passion); and CPEB:CW, IV/4.6 (1789 Passion).

Example 2.6. C. P. E. Bach's parody aria "Erfrecht euch nur, die Unschuld zu verklagen" (1789 Passion, no. 19), with his sketch (D-B, SA 5136, fol. 28v).

Bach's strategy offers a more natural presentation of the poetry, closer to how one would speak the text.

Far from a mere shortcut born of laziness, borrowing for Bach entailed work. As one examines the details of his meticulous approach to selecting and applying procedures for revising existing material for use in his Passions, Bach's studious nature emerges. The pervasiveness of his changes to both texts and musical settings among these borrowed works suggests that they stem from the same drive—or "restlessness," to borrow Rachel Wade's term—that distinguished Bach's attitude toward his own works.[35] In fact, the manner in which David Schulenberg has described the composer's method

35. See Rachel W. Wade, "Carl Philipp Emanuel Bach, the Restless Composer," in *Carl Philipp Emanuel Bach und die europäische Musikkultur des mittleren 18. Jahrhunderts*, ed. Hans Joachim Marx (Göttingen: Vandenhoeck and Ruprecht, 1990), 175–88.

Table 2.11. Text of Homilius, "Verdammt ihn nur, ihr ungerechten Richter"
(HoWV I.10, no. 23), and parody text, "Erfrecht euch nur,
die Unschuld zu verklagen" (1789 Passion, no. 19)

Homilius, HoWV I.10, no. 23	Bach, 1789 Passion, no. 19
Verdammt ihn nur, ihr ungerechten Richter,	Erfrecht euch nur, die Unschuld zu verklagen
Verdammt ihn nur,	Und sprecht dem Sohn
Den Schöpfer der Natur!	Des großen Schöpfers Hohn!
Wenn einst die Welt ins erste Nichts zurücke fällt,	Gestreckt zu seinen Füßen,
Wenn dann der Sohn als Richter	Verworfne, müßt ihr ewiglich
In Wolken sein Gerichte hält,	Für eure Bosheit büßen.
Dann flieht, ihr Bösewichter!	
Go ahead and condemn him, you unjust judges,	*Just you dare and accuse Innocence himself,*
Go ahead and condemn the one	*And mock the son*
Who created nature!	*Of the great creator!*
When the world reverts to its former nothingness,	*Stretched out before his feet,*
When the son then	*You rejected ones must eternally*
Administers justice in the clouds as judge,	*Atone for your wickedness.*
Then flee, you evildoers!	

of "renovating" his *own* compositions ("something more than a superficial revision" in which "movements were expanded . . . alongside drastic alterations of the melodic material") describes well Bach's approach to some of the borrowings from other composers examined here.[36]

Beyond meeting practical obligations tied to the circumstances of performance or necessitated by borrowing itself, Bach's sensitive treatment of the musical and poetic substance of the works he encountered and shared with the Hamburg public served as an outlet for creativity and an avenue to apply his developing aesthetic goals. Certain patterns of revision in his treatment of borrowed material suggest that an evolving set of underlying principles different from those of the previous generation guided his choices. Examples of this sort include the shift away from strict da capo form, the shrinking of ritornelli, the reduction of melismatic text setting, and a favoring of more natural text declamation, among others. These unambiguously indicate a dissolution of those aesthetic standards more closely associated with the baroque and instead point toward the development of a new paradigm.

36. David Schulenberg, *The Music of Carl Philipp Emanuel Bach* (Rochester: University of Rochester Press, 2014), 25.

Table 2.12. Text repetitions used for Homilius, "Verdammt ihn nur" (1770 Passion, no. 13), and for parody version, "Erfrecht euch nur" (1789 Passion, no. 19)

Homilius, HoWV I.10, no. 23; Bach, 1770 Passion, no. 13	Bach, 1789 Passion, no. 19
[ritornello]	[short ritornello]
Verdammt ihn nur,	Erfrecht euch nur,
ihr ungerechten Richter	die Unschuld zu verklagen,
verdammt ihn nur,	und sprecht dem Sohn
den Schöpfer der Natur,	des großen Schöpfers Hohn!
den Schöpfer der Natur	Erfrecht euch nur,
Ihr ungerechten Richter,	die Unschuld zu verkla—gen [4 mm.]
verda—mmt [6 mm.] ihn nur	und sprecht dem Sohn
den Schöpfer der Natur,	des großen Schöfpers Hohn!
verdammt ihn nur,	
ihr ungerechten Richter,	
verdammt ihn nur,	
verdammt ihn nur,	
verdammt ihn nur,	
den Schöpfer der Natur!	
[ritornello]	[short ritornello]
Verdammt ihn nur,	Erfrecht euch nur,
ihr ungerechten Richter,	die Unschuld zu verklagen,
verdammt ihn nur,	und sprecht dem Sohn
verdammt ihn nur,	des großen Schöpfers Hohn!
verdammt ihn nur,	Erfrecht euch nur, erfrecht euch,
verdammt ihn,	die Unschuld zu verklagen,
den Schöpfer der Natur	und sprecht dem Sohn
verda—mmt [3 mm.] ihn,	des großen Schöpfers Hohn,
verda—mmt [3 mm.] ihn	des großen Schöpfers Hohn!
verda—mmt ihn nur,	
den Schöpfer der Natur,	
ungerechten Richter,	
ihr ungerechten Richter	
verdammt ihn nur,	
verdammt ihn,	
den Schöpfer der Natur,	
verdammt ihn nur,	
den Schöpfer,	
den Schöpfer der Natur!	
[ritornello]	[short ritornello]
Wenn einst die Welt	Gestreckt zu seinen Füßen,
ins erste Nichts zurücke fällt,	Verworfne, müßt ihr ewiglich
wenn dann der Sohn als Richter	für eure Bosheit büßen.
in Wolken sein Gerichte hält,	Gestreckt zu seinen Füßen,
dann flieht, ihr Bösewichter,	gestreckt zu seinen Füßen,
dann flieht, ihr Bösewichter,	Verworfne, müßt ihr ewiglich
dann flieht,	für eure Bosheit büßen,
dann flieht, ihr Bösewichter!	für eure Bosheit büßen.
flieht,	
dann flieht, ihr Bösewichter!	
[ritornello] da capo	da capo

The Bach-Busoni
Goldberg Variations

Erinn E. Knyt

I n the preface to his 1915 edition of Johann Sebastian Bach's "Aria mit 30 Veränderungen" (Goldberg Variations, BWV 988) for solo piano, Ferruccio Busoni
(1866–1924) called the piece the most "copious" and "ingenious" of Bach's sets
of variations.[1] Yet, he believed the composition could not be performed successfully
on the piano without modification and that it needed to be adapted for contemporary
listeners. His arrangement, as he stated, set about to "rescue this remarkable work for
the concert-hall."[2] Busoni's modifications included shortening the piece by nine variations, creating an overall sense of architectural form by grouping the variations into
three main sections with a climax at the end of the second section, and transcribing
the composition for the piano. He did this by changing time signatures, redistributing
notes between the hands, altering rhythmic values, and changing pitches.

Scholars have largely overlooked Busoni's adaptation of the Goldberg Variations,
instead reserving more detailed analyses for his transcriptions of the Chaconne from

1. I am grateful to Tzimon Barto and Chiyan Wong for sharing their insights about the Busoni
version of the Goldberg Variations with me. Thanks are also due Pam Juengling for her assistance
in tracking down rare editions of the Goldberg Variations, to Ernest May and Brent Auerbach for
their comments on a draft of this essay, and to Alan Walker for sharing his knowledge about Liszt
and the Goldberg Variations. Bridget Carr (Boston Symphony Archives) also deserves thanks for her
assistance in locating the photograph of Busoni at his harpsichord, and Jean-Christophe Gero was
helpful locating archival materials at the Staatsbibliothek zu Berlin. Earlier versions of this essay were
presented at the American Bach Society meeting in New Haven, Connecticut (Yale University), in
April 2018, at the University of Warsaw in May 2018, and at the National Meeting of the American
Musicological Society in Boston in November 2019.

Ferruccio Busoni, preface to Johann Sebastian Bach, *Aria mit 30 Veränderungen (Goldbergsche Variationen)*, ed. Busoni, vol. 15, *Klavierwerke* (Leipzig: Breitkopf & Härtel, 1915), trans. Mevanwy Roberts,
1–8 (quote on 1).

2. Ibid., 3.

the Partita No. 2 for Solo Violin in D Minor, BWV 1004, and of organ chorale preludes, for instance.[3] This neglect can perhaps be attributed to the liberal way Busoni modified Bach's Goldberg Variations; he not only transcribed the piece but also reworked it to reflect the taste of his own age. Although such practices were not uncommon in relation to Bach's music, they had not previously been applied to the Goldberg Variations. Busoni's revised work thus may not represent Bach's intentions, but it was an important early attempt to resurrect this work in an era in which it was rarely performed. By contextualizing an analysis of Busoni's edition and performances of the Goldberg Variations within a reception history of the piece, my essay also contributes to ongoing discourse about the evolution of performance practice of Bach's keyboard compositions. In so doing, it reveals changing attitudes about textual fidelity and the role of the interpreter in the twenty-first century.

Performance History

In a 1986 *New York Times* article, Tim Page quoted Charles Rosen, whose statement about Busoni's Goldberg Variations summed up the prevailing attitude of many performers in the mid- to late twentieth century—namely, that some early twentieth-century performers (like Busoni) represented an era in which performers overstepped Bach's intentions. Rosen, who was an advocate of letting the notation speak for itself, exclaimed that it would be unthinkable for any of his contemporaries to play similarly, making specific reference to the powerful ending of the Busoni version: "Ferruccio Busoni's Bach arrangements offer some fascinating examples in the history of taste.... At the end of the *Goldberg Variations*, for example, he simply couldn't allow the theme to return unadorned; he had to thunder it out as a chorale. I don't think anybody would get away with this today, but it's very much of its time."[4]

Rosen's comment reflects a veneration of textual fidelity, a notion of how to show allegiance to the composer's intentions, and a preference for viewing the performer as mainly an interpreter.[5] Yet these attitudes about textual fidelity were just develop-

3. See, for instance, Roman Vlad, "I Preludi Corali di Bach nella trascrizione di Busoni," in *La Trascrizione Bach e Busoni*, ed. Talia Pecker Berio, *Quaderni della Rivista italiana di musicologia*, 18 (Florence: Leo S. Olschki, 1987), 3–21; and Talia Pecker Berio, "La *Chaconne* e i suoi visitatori," in *Trascrizione Bach e Busoni*, 59–82. Larry Sitsky devotes only one page to the arrangement: Larry Sitsky, *Busoni and the Piano: The Works, the Writings, and the Recordings*, 2nd ed., Pendragon Distinguished Reprints, no. 3 (Hillsdale, N.Y.: Pendragon Press, 2009), 194.

4. Charles Rosen, interview by Tim Page, "A Pianist Makes Bach His Instrument," *New York Times*, 8 June 1986.

5. See the following texts for late twentieth-century literature about these performance trends: Raymond Leppert, *Authenticity in Music* (Portland, Ore.: Amadeus Press, 1988); Nicholas Kenyon, ed.,

ing while Busoni was preparing his version of Bach's Goldberg Variations in 1914. It was a relatively obscure work at that time with few performances. Even so, Busoni's arrangement took more liberties than other versions of the Goldberg Variations.[6] The first documented performance in the nineteenth century might be a two-piano arrangement, improvised during a private performance in Charles Burney's home by Samuel Wesley and Vincent Novello in 1810.[7] According to Philip Olleson, the two decided to bring an extra grand piano to Burney's home for the performance since a harpsichord was not available.[8] Burney suggested—due to the piece's length—that it be performed in three segments, but Wesley objected on the grounds that the piece needed to be appreciated as a whole. They played the entire piece from start to finish. Franz Liszt was perhaps the first to perform the variations publicly on solo piano, although little is known about his performances, including whether he performed the variations in part or whole, which edition he used, and whether he altered them in any way.[9] August Conradi (one of Liszt's assistants in Weimar), who compiled a list of Liszt's repertoire, included the Goldberg Variations among the pieces that Liszt played during those years of concertizing.[10] Alan Walker maintains, "There is no doubt that

---

Authenticity and Early Music (New York: Oxford University Press, 1988); David Schulenberg, "Expression and Authenticity in the Harpsichord Music of J. S. Bach," *Journal of Musicology* 8 (1990): 449–76; Lydia Goehr, *The Imaginary Museum of Musical Works: An Essay in the Philosophy of Music* (Oxford: Clarendon Press, 1992); Leo Treitler, *Music and the Historical Imagination* (Cambridge, Mass.: Harvard University Press, 1989); Richard Taruskin, *Text and Act: Essays on Music Performance* (New York: Oxford University Press, 1995).

6. Although other performers, such as Franz Liszt, had already made numerous transcriptions of the music of Bach, the Goldberg Variations had not been so freely arranged before Busoni.

7. For more information about this performance, see Philip Olleson, "Dr. Burney, Samuel Wesley, and J. S. Bach's Goldberg Variations," in *The Rosaleen Moldenhauer Memorial: Music History from Primary Sources. A Guide to the Moldenhauer Archives*, ed. Jon Newsom and Alfred Mann (Washington, D.C.: Library of Congress, 2000), 169–75. The performance took place on 20 July 1810 on Burney's Broadwood grand pianoforte and another similar instrument.

8. Wesley might have performed from the Nägeli edition: *Variationen für das Klavier* (Zurich: Nägeli, c. 1800). The other available edition was *Exercices pour le clavecin* (Vienna and Leipzig: Hoffmeister, 1803). Wesley might also have performed from his personal copy of the manuscript; see Olleson, "Dr. Burney," 174. His copy of the manuscript is now in the British Library, Add MS 14344, fols. 59–81.

9. For more information about Franz Liszt's relationship to the music of J. S. Bach, see Michael Heinemann, *Die Bach-Rezeption von Franz Liszt*, Musik und Musikanschauung im 19. Jahrhundert, ed. Detlef Altenburg, vol. 1 (Cologne: Studio, 1995).

10. The list was titled "Programme général des morceaux exécutés par F. Liszt à ses concerts de 1838 à 1848." The document may be consulted in the Goethe- und Schiller-Archiv in Weimar under the shelf mark GSA 60/Z 15.

Conradi received this information directly from Liszt himself."[11] However, Walker also notes that he has viewed many printed programs of Liszt's concerts and has not yet seen one mentioning the Goldberg Variations.[12] It is further known that Liszt talked about the piece with his students, such as José Vianna da Motta, a close friend of Busoni. Da Motta performed the piece on solo piano for Liszt's master class in Weimar in 1885 and again publicly in Berlin in 1908 using the arrangement by Karl Klindworth, another Liszt pupil.[13] It may be presumed that Klindworth also played the variations—at least in private—while he created his arrangement in 1902.

At the turn of the century, there was also a revival of the piece in England, as part of a more general early music revival. Alfred Hipkins demonstrated at least part of the variations for the Royal Musical Association on the harpsichord in 1886.[14] A more complete performance is described in the *Musical Times* in 1898: "He played all the two-keyboard variations in his later lectures, with the *gallantly* treated aria, of course, and the Quodlibet. It is almost certain that they were never played on a harpsichord before in this country."[15] Harold Samuel, a Bach specialist, performed the piece repeatedly on piano, including in 1898 in London at his debut recital.[16] Harold Schonberg describes one of Samuel's later New York performances from the 1930s, noting its adherence to the text and steadiness of tempo: "His Bach playing was of the utmost

---

11. Alan Walker, e-mail message to author, 22 July 2017.

12. Ibid.

13. José Vianna da Motta, "Liszt as Teacher: A Sketch by José Vianna da Motta," in *The Piano Master Classes of Franz Liszt, 1884–1886: Diary Notes of August Göllerich*, ed. Wilhelm Jerger, trans. and enlarged by Richard Louis Zimdars (Bloomington: Indiana University Press, 2010), appendix B (from *Der Merker*, October 1911). Also see the following account in "Berlin," *Musical Courier: A Weekly Journal Devoted to Music* 56 (18 January 1908): 5: "Jose Vianna da Motta gave two interesting recitals at Beethoven Hall, affording his numerous auditors keen enjoyment. Da Motta is not only a great pianist, but he is also an exceedingly clever musician, and he always offers something new and interesting. At his first recital he played, among other things, Klindworth's effective arrangement of the Bach-Goldberg Variations, the Beethoven sonata, op. 106, and the Schumann symphonic etudes with the five posthumous variations."

14. Cyril Ehrlich, "Alfred Hipkins," *Grove Music Online*, accessed 16 July 2017, http://www.oxford musiconline.com/subscriber/article/grove/music/13069.

15. "Alfred James Hipkins," *Musical Times* 39 (1 September 1898): 581–86 (quote on 585). For more information about the English Bach movement, see F. G. E[dwards], "Bach's Music in England," *Musical Times* 37 (1896): 585–87, 652–57, 722–26, 797–800.

16. Compton Pakenham, "Newly Recorded Music," *New York Times*, 24 December 1933. See also "Goldberg Variations Played by Samuel: Work Lasting 43 Minutes Given in Third of Bach Series at the Town Hall," *New York Times*, 10 January 1935; and David Dubal, *The Art of the Piano: Its Performers, Literature, and Recordings* (Pompton Plains, N.J.: Amadeus Press, 2004).

elegance, flexibility, transparency and logic. He reflected the modern style in its lack of elaborate, Busoni-like ritards, in its strict adherence to the text, and in its rhythmic steadiness."[17] Sir Donald Francis Tovey likewise performed the variations in 1904— presumably on solo piano. This is documented by an inscription in the front of Tovey's personal copy of a composition by Otto Goldschmidt, who wrote, "Donald Fr. Tovey in grateful remembrance of a great musical treet [*sic*]—his playing of Seb. Bach's 30 Variations from the composer Otto Goldschmidt London December 15, 1904."[18] Although there are no descriptions of the performance or surviving recordings, Tovey left an essay about the Goldberg Variations stating his view that Bach's music should follow the notation as written (without extra doublings) on the piano but should take full advantage of the piano's expressive capabilities:

> The nearest possible translation from the language of the harpsichord to that of the modern pianoforte is here, as in almost all cases, to play the music exactly as it is written, but to use the fullness of tone that one's fingers can produce. The genius of the pianoforte is to make gradations and "colors" of tone by touch; the genius of the harpsichord is to do the same by 4- and 16-foot registers, "lute stops," and the like; deficiencies in the finer details of cantabile expression being supplied by the imagination of the sympathetic listener.[19]

Around the same time as Liszt's performances, editions of the piece for solo piano also appeared, such as Carl Czerny's edition from 1840 "for piano alone."[20] The overall legato touch indicated by slurs, finger substitutions, and more, as well as the numerous dynamic and affect markings, suggests he was aiming for a very pianistic rendering. Hans Bischoff likewise created a solo piano edition.[21] Although more scholarly than Czerny's and more varied in articulation, Bischoff's edition occasionally suggested

17. Harold Schonberg, *The Great Pianists from Mozart to the Present* (New York: Simon and Schuster, 2006), 410.

18. Otto Goldschmidt, *Three Pianoforte Pieces, op. 25, no. 3: Variations on a Theme by Johann Sebastian Bach* (London: Edmond Ashdown, n.d.). The inscription is written on the verso of the cover of the exemplar at University of Edinburgh, Main Library (StEdU: Tov. 628/2); the inscription is transcribed in the library's catalog entry for this item at https://discovered.ed.ac.uk (accessed 26 April 2019).

19. Donald Francis Tovey, "Aria with Thirty Variations (The 'Goldberg' Variations)" (1900), in *The Goldberg Reader: A Performer's Guide and Anthology of Critical Appreciation*, ed. Laurette Goldberg with Jonathan Rhode Lee (Berkeley: MusiSources, 1978), 21–38 (quote on 23).

20. J. S. Bach, *Thème avec 30 Variations*, ed. Carl Czerny, Friedrich Conrad Griepenkerl, and Friedrich August Roitzsch (Leipzig: C. F. Peters, c. 1850). It is possible that Liszt could have performed from this version.

21. J. S. Bach, *Joh. Seb. Bach's Clavierwerke*, Vierter Band, ed. Hans Bischoff (Hannover: Steingräber), 1883.

alternate note distributions for variations originally written for two manuals. One can only wonder if Klindworth's edition, which contains very few explanatory notes, reflected Liszt's performances or teachings about the piece.[22] Klindworth did recommend that pianists perform the variations without repeats in public.[23] He also suggested an overall legato touch and added the una corda pedal in Variation 13 and the sostenuto pedal in Variation 16. Other adjustments took the form of a few doublings, such as at the conclusion of Variation 8. In Variation 17, Klindworth displaced notes in the bass (one octave lower) and added extra pitches beginning in measure 5. Josef Rheinberger likewise published a two-piano adaptation in 1883, which Max Reger revised in 1915. Rheinberger's version is a freer adaptation with octave doublings and enriched chords, in addition to note redistributions between the two pianos and indications to use the pedal for a richer sound. Karl Eichler's two-piano version from 1912 displays only minor textual changes.

Public performances and editions of the Goldberg Variations before Busoni's time were thus not common but were becoming more frequent. They included a variety of approaches in terms of instrument, number of performers, portion of the work performed, the use of pedal, and ideas about touch, not to mention ornamentation.

Busoni's Arrangement

Busoni's published arrangement of the Goldberg Variations in 1915 and his first performances of the work in late 1914 thus occurred when there was burgeoning interest in the piece, even if it was still not well known and had few defined performance traditions. Despite this, Busoni's version was by far the most liberal. It stood in the somewhat ambiguous region between an edition, a transcription, and an arrangement. Like Czerny, Bischoff, Klindworth, and others, Busoni was trying to make the work appropriate for the piano, but he did so in his own way, even studying the harpsichord and considering ways to preserve the textures, power, and colors of the harpsichord on the modern piano—and without resorting to the use of two pianos, as Reger and Rheinberger had done. Moreover, he went beyond Bach in places by changing the pitches and even the overall structure. He frequently crossed back and forth between roles of editor, composer, transcriber, and performer, leaving it up to the performer to make the final decisions by including multiple options in the score. The result was an open edition that offered many possibilities from which the performer could choose.

---

22. Klindworth also taught in London for fourteen years, where he worked with Alfred Hipkins.

23. Johann Sebastian Bach, *Aria with 30 Variations*, ed. Karl Klindworth (Leipzig: Breitkopf & Härtel, 1902), 2.

Busoni's arrangement of the Goldberg Variations was a by-product of his work on an edition of the complete keyboard works of J. S. Bach.[24] He divided up the editing tasks with Egon Petri and Bruno Mugellini, reserving what he found most interesting for himself.[25] It was only after starting on the editing project that he added the Goldberg Variations to his performance repertoire, and he reworked the piece for his personal use, initially trying it out in a recital the fall before the printed version of his arrangement appeared. His first performance of the piece took place on October 10, 1914, in Berlin during an all-Bach recital. He started with the Organ Prelude and Triple Fugue in E-flat Major, BWV 552, and ended with the Goldberg Variations (see Figure 3.1). The ambitious program also included the Capriccio on the Departure of a Beloved Brother, BWV 992, and the Prelude, Fugue, and Allegro, BWV 998 (originally for harpsichord or lute).[26]

If one of Busoni's aims was to make the Goldberg Variations more accessible, it seems that he was successful. A newspaper review of that first performance stated that the hall was full and the applause enthusiastic.[27] Another review applauded him for making the variations more accessible to audiences. It maintained that before Busoni, the variations were considered "dreaded" and "outlandishly heavy":

> The Goldberg Variations would probably have frightened many without the prospect of hearing them in the new Busonian arrangement performed by the master himself. Now that Busoni has played these dreaded variations, one has to admit that they are quite different from listening to them on two pianos or trying to play them on one's own. It is doubtful whether Count von Kayserling's [sic] melancholy really waned when the young Goldberg played the variations for him, some of which are and remain boring. On the other hand, the great beauty of individual variations stands out more clearly, such as . . . in the 25th, which was performed by Busoni with touching

24. For more information about the edition and about Busoni's editing process, see Chiara Bertoglio, "Instructive Editions of Bach's *Wohltemperirtes Klavier*: An Italian Perspective" (Ph.D., University of Birmingham, 2012), 216–22. Bertoglio explored Busoni's arrangement of the Goldberg Variations in her lecture-recital, "Enhancing the Spectacular: Busoni on Bach's Goldberg Variations," Bach Network UK, Dialogue Meeting, Cambridge, England, 8–10 July 2015, and has recorded the work on *Bach & Italy, Vol. 1: Marcello, Brahms, Busoni*, Da Vinci Classics 7.93588765521, 2018, compact disc. A live performance of the piece by Bertoglio (23 November 2017) is also available online; accessed 26 April 2019, https://www.youtube.com/watch?v=6TrMEw8Lbmo.

25. Busoni, letter of 23 August 1910 to Egon Petri, in *Ferruccio Busoni: Selected Letters*, trans. and ed. Antony Beaumont (New York: Columbia University Press, 1987), 111–12.

26. In his diary Busoni wrote that the Bach recital was causing him some anxiety, and he was relieved when it was well received. See Busoni, diary entry of 10 October 1914, in *Ferruccio Busoni: Selected Letters*, 188.

27. "Busoni als Bach-Spieler," *Vossische Zeitung* (Berlin), 14 October 1914.

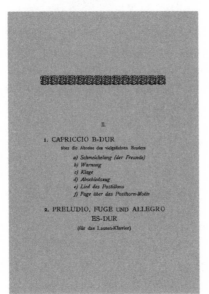

Figure 3.1. Recital program from Busoni's first performance of his arrangement of Bach's Goldberg Variations, October 10, 1914, Berlin Singakademie. Staatsbibliothek zu Berlin—Preußischer Kulturbesitz, Musikabteilung mit Mendelssohn-Archiv, Mus. Nachl. F. Busoni E 1914, 18. Reproduced with permission.

tenderness, the 28th, with a play on Beethoven's op. 109, the Beethovenesque 29th Variation, and the very exquisite Quodlibet. Reliable information about the Busoni arrangement will, of course, be communicated when it is published. . . . The number of thirty variations appears reduced by ten. One must have heard with what grace and clarity Busoni plays the outlandishly heavy pieces! From memory![28]

His choice to perform without any repeats further shortened the piece, making it easier on listeners.

He subsequently performed the variations multiple times in Germany, England, Switzerland, and Italy, always in his arranged version. One of his students from the Bologna Conservatory, Guido Agosti, witnessed his performance of the Goldberg Variations in 1922 in Milan, noting that he programmed it together with Ludwig van Beethoven's "Hammerklavier Sonata": "I heard Busoni again, about two years before his death, in Milano. These were the last two recitals he gave in Italy and these I will always remember. I was about twenty-two. In the first program he played the *Goldberg Variations*, a group of his own pieces, and Beethoven's Opus 106. In the second program, he played the *Waldstein Sonata*, Chopin's four *Ballades*, and the two Liszt *Legends of St. Francis*. It was absolutely unbelievable."[29]

If audiences in German-speaking lands and in Italy were largely supportive of Busoni's arrangement, there must have been some criticism in London, which had already heard performances of more complete versions of the piece on harpsichord. One of Busoni's staunchest admirers, Edward Dent, felt the need to defend Busoni's arrangement after a performance in London in 1919. In particular, it seems that there

---

28. Siegmund Pisling, "Aus Berlin: Ein Bachabend," *Signale für die Musikalische Welt* 41 (14 October 1914): 1345:

> Die Goldbergvariationen hätten wohl viele abgeschreckt ohne die Aussicht, sie in der neuen Busonischen Bearbeitung und vom Meister selbst zu hören. Jetzt, wo Busoni diese gefürchteten Variationen gespielt hat, muss man zugeben, dass sie doch ganz anders wirken, als wenn man sie auf zwei Klavieren hört oder ihnen mit den eignen zehn Fingern beizukommen sucht. Man hegt zwar auch jetzt Zweifel, ob der Trübsinn des Freiherrn von Kayserling [sic] auch wirklich schwand, wenn ihn der junge Goldberg die Variationen vorspielte, denn manche darunter sind und bleiben langweilig. Dafür tritt die hohe Schönheit einzelner Variationen um so klarer hervor, so . . . der 25., die von Busoni mit rührender Innigkeit gesungen wurde, der 28., mit Fingern auf op. 109 von Beethoven weisenden, der ebenfalls beethovenischen 29. Variation und des ganz köstlichen Quodlibets. Verlässliches über die Busoni'sche Bearbeitung wird man natürlich erst mitteilen können, wenn sie gedruckt ist. . . . Die Zahl von dreissig Veränderungen erscheint um zehn verringert. Man muss gehört haben, mit welcher Anmut und Klarheit Busoni die haarsträubend schweren Stücke spielt! Auswendig spielt!

29. Guido Agosti, "Guido Agosti—Busoni Pupil," interviewed by Daniel M. Raessler, *Piano Quarterly* 108.28 (Winter 1979–80): 55–56.

were objections to his use of the piano, the pedal, and the power with which he played the piece. Surprisingly, Dent did not feel the need to justify his elimination of nine of the variations:

> If you do not like the way in which Busoni plays the "Goldberg" variations, the originals are always to your hand and you may go home and play them for yourself—if you can. He has no wish to reproduce for you the tinkle of the harpsichord. Yet he knows the harpsichord and its peculiar personality, knows that to Bach it meant not a tender and fragrant evocation of a quaint and ghostly past, but the loud and clangerous assertion of a hard and definite present. That is why he plays Bach with a firm metallic tone that rings clear and trumpet-like through the reverberations which the pedal has released.[30]

Busoni considered the Goldberg Variations to be Bach's most ingenious set of variations, but not his most perfect—and he set about to make them a little bit better, in his estimation:

> The Passacaglia for Organ, the Ciaconna for Violin, and the 30 Variations are the three great examples of Bach's art of Variation. Of the three, the Passacaglia appears to me to be the most perfect, but the 30 Variations are certainly both the most copious and the most ingenious.—Among the Pianoforte works of the master, they hold an important place, between the "Well tempered Clavichord" (The 48 Preludes) and Fugues and the Chromatic Fantasy, without, however, equaling the one in exuberant variety, or the other in poetic freedom.[31]

Busoni's "improvements" include changes to the structure of the piece. He created a three-movement structure with a climax near the end by grouping the variations into three sets: Variations 1–13 (discarding nos. 3, 9, and 12); Variations 14–25 (discarding nos. 16, 17, 18, 21, and 24);[32] and Variations 26–30 (discarding no. 27). The final aria, according to Busoni, should be played without ornamentation and with note doublings to differentiate it from the opening aria.

---

30. Edward Dent, "Busoni and the Pianoforte," *Athenaeum* 4669 (24 October 1919), 1072–73. Dent's article was written in response to Busoni's recital on 15 October 1919 in London, which included the following pieces: Bach, Goldberg Variations; Beethoven, Sonata, op. 106; and a few compositions by Liszt. Other letters documenting Busoni's own impressions of his performances include the following: Busoni, letters of 9 October 1919 and 15 October 1919 to Gerda Busoni, in Busoni, *Letters to his Wife*, trans. Rosamond Ley (London: Edward Arnold and Co., 1938), 272; and Busoni, letter of 21 October 1919 to Volkmar Andreae, in *Ferruccio Busoni: Selected Letters*, 294.

31. Busoni, preface to *Aria mit 30 Veränderungen*, 1. It is worth noting that the Passacaglia and the Ciaconna are already tripartite works.

32. Busoni suggested, however, that Variation 17 could, alternatively, be substituted for Variation 14.

In addition, he suggested linking certain of the variations together to create a larger structural feel, such as launching into Variation 10 without a pause (attacca). He justified some of the groupings by claiming motivic similarities. For instance, he showed motivic connections between Variations 10 and 11, writing them out on four staves (see Example 3.1).[33] One of the more dramatic groupings was the coda consisting of the Allegro finale, the Quodlibet, and the Aria ripresa with stark octave doublings and no ornamentation to bring the piece to a powerful conclusion (see Example 3.2).

These changes represent a major shift from the piece as Bach envisioned it, with the Overture (Variation 16) serving as the center of a bipartite piece. Busoni claimed this tripartite structure as he envisioned it had metaphysical significance: "The division into groups signifies, not only a breathing pause, an arrangement of the sections, a synopsis: it personifies also three distinct conditions of creative production; interplay within the circle; inward penetration; outward exaltation." This passage references many of the aesthetic concepts that Busoni explains in more detail in his writings and letters. It is probable that the "circle" mentioned here refers to the circle of Bach's creative activity.[34] In an essay written shortly before he died, Busoni explained that the greatest compositional giants carve out their own circle of influence within this great and vast sphere of music. Other composers (even from other time periods) can penetrate and identify with the composer's circle, as Busoni did with Bach's in his arrangement of the Goldberg Variations:

> Even to the greatest giant, the circle in which his activity unfolds must remain a limited one. However much he may grasp, in relation to the infinity out of which he

---

33. "Innerhalb einzelner Gruppen sollte eine Variation aus der vorhergegangen herauswachsen. Der konstruktive Zusammenhang dieser Veränderung mit der Fughetta ist aus der Möglichkeit ersichtlich, durch welche die Motive der beiden übereinandergestellt werden." Busoni, *Aria mit 30 Veränderungen*, 22.

34. Busoni, preface to *Aria mit 30 Veränderungen*, 4. Some of Busoni's writings can be found in his *The Essence of Music and Other Papers*, trans. Rosamond Ley (London: Rockliff, 1957). Some of his aesthetic ideas have also been discussed in more detail in Martina Weindel, *Ferruccio Busonis Aesthetik in seinen Briefen und Schriften*, ed. Richard Schaal (Wilhelmshaven: Noetzel, 1996); and Erinn Knyt, "'How I Compose': Ferruccio Busoni's Views about Invention, Quotation, and the Compositional Process," *Journal of Musicology* 27.2 (2010): 224–64.

However, Busoni's idea of the circle has not yet been discussed in detail. Busoni frequently used shapes to describe his concepts. The circle was a symbol that permeates his writings and also refers to completeness and multi-sidedness. He uses a circle to illustrate the concept of the "horizon of sound" that he envisioned in theater; see "The Score of *Doktor Faust*," in the *Essence of Music*, 70–76 (quote on 73). The circle also signifies wholeness and the protection of magic to a Faust who is vulnerable only when he steps outside of the circle (72). Busoni describes music as flora covering the whole earth (circle) yet also extending beyond to the entire universe (see "The Essence of Music: A Paving of the Way to an Understanding of the Everlasting Calendar," in *Essence of Music*, 193–200, esp. 197).

Example 3.1. Busoni's Goldberg Variations, Busoni's conflation of Variations 10 and 11

creates it, is bound to be a tiny particle; just as the highest ascent takes us no nearer to the sun. Inside this radius, ruled by one person and restricted for him in time and place by the chances of his birth, the individual mind feels especially drawn through a natural sympathy to particular points and cultures, while his nature is placed in closer relationship with certain details, owing to similar distinctive qualities. The creative artist favours these points so much that he gladly and frequently returns to them in his works.[35]

35. Busoni, "Essence of Music," 197.

Example 3.2. Busoni's Goldberg Variations, concluding Aria, mm. 1–8.

The three parts of the Goldberg Variations, according to Busoni, therefore seem to represent growth, from a play with the themes and materials that Busoni discovered in Bach's "circle of musical activity," to a discovery and exploration of their hidden and inner meanings and possibilities, to an external celebration of those musical materials in Busoni's own style that culminates in the bold final aria.

Another major structural shift was Busoni's insistence that the work should be thought of as containing two different types of variations: virtuosic and contrapuntal, as opposed to the Bachian groupings of three types (dance-like, virtuosic, and canonic). He allowed for only four exceptions: the Gigue (Variation 7), an Andante (Variation 13), the French Overture (Variation 16), and an Adagio (Variation 25): "The 30 Variations divide up into 'pianistic' and 'imitatory,'—(Piano studies, and contrapunctal [*sic*] studies)—, intersected by four 'detached': a Gigue, an Andante, an Overture after the French model, ('French Overture,' which consists of two kinds of Variations in succession), and an Adagio; this last, the most remarkable, and most beautiful piece of the collection, being the one which invites the comparison with Beethoven alluded to;—this, with two other 'imitative' Variations, forms a subdivision of three movements in the minor mode."[36] Busoni's list of "imitatory" variations included not only the canons but also fughettas, the Quodlibet, and any other contrapuntal or imitative variations, including the opening section of the Overture (Variation 16) (see Table 3.1).

Busoni reshaped the piece not only through this new conception of the variations but also by suggesting the elimination of nine variations (nos. 3, 9, 12, 14 or 17, 16,

36. Busoni, preface to *Aria mit 30 Veränderungen*, 1.

Table 3.1. Busoni's List of Imitatory Variations

Variation 2. Free imitation, 3-part
Variation 3. Canon at the unison
Variation 4. Free imitation, 4-part
Variation 6. Canon at the second
Variation 9. Canon at the third
Variation 10. Fughetta I
Variation 12. Canon at the fourth (in contrary motion)
Variation 15. Canon at the fifth (in contrary motion, and in minor)
Variation 16. Fughetta II (Allegro of the Overture)
Variation 18. Canon at the sixth
Variation 19. Free imitation, 3-part
Variation 21. Canon at the seventh (and in minor)
Variation 22. Fugato, 4-part
Variation 24. Canon at the octave
Variation 27. Canon at the ninth, 2-part
Variation 30. Quodlibet

18, 21, 24, 27), most of them contrapuntal, thereby placing greater weight on the virtuosic variations. Busoni also suggested that Variation 17 could be performed in place of Variation 14, which is the way he played the piece. (See Table 3.2.) This choice to remove so many contrapuntal variations might seem puzzling for a composer who wrote continually about the value of counterpoint as a fundamental basis for his own compositions and for the music of the future as he envisioned it.[37] His mature works often feature canons and fugues, such as in the *Fantasia Contrappuntistica*, which climaxes with a grand and lengthy fugue. However, Busoni's own compositional approach frequently blends Bachian counterpoint with Beethovenian drama, climaxes, and scope—something it appears that he hoped to blend into his version of Bach's Goldberg Variations as well. Rather than alternating canons with virtuoso variations so predictably as Bach had done, he interspersed a few contrapuntal variations to help build a sense of climax on a larger scale in his new arrangement. For instance, Busoni's dramatized arrangement of the Quodlibet (Variation 30) follows directly after his Beethovenian arrangement of the virtuosic Variation 29, thereby increasing the tension and contributing to a dramatic final resolution in the bold concluding aria.

It is important to note, however, that Busoni's arrangement is an open one, leaving many decisions up to the performer. Just as he believed that he had penetrated Bach's

37. See, for instance, Busoni's letter to Paul Bekker of January 1920, in which he proclaimed the need for the art of the future to return to melody and "the most highly developed (not the most complicated) polyphony," in *Essence of Music*, 19–22 (quote on 21).

Table 3.2. The Variations Busoni Played from
the Goldberg Variations

Aria
First Group (Movement I):
  1. Allegro (1)
  2. Andantino (2)
  3. Lo stesso movimento (4)
  4. Allegro non troppo (5)
  5. Canone alla Seconda (6)
  6. Allegro Scherzando (7)
  7. Allegro (8)
  8. Fughetta (10)
  9. Più vivace (11)
  10. Andante con grazia (13)
Second Group (Movement II):
  11. Allegro ritenuto (14, or instead, Allegro slanciato [17])
  12. Canone alla Quinta (15)
  13. Allegretto piacevole (19)
  14. Allegretto vivace (20)
  15. Fugato (22)
  16. Non allegro (23)
  17. Adagio (25)
Third Group (Movement III):
  18. Allegro corrente (26)
  19. Andante brilliante (28)
  20. Allegro finale (29)
  21. Quodlibet (30)
Ripresa (Aria)

"circle of artistic activity," he hoped that those who followed him would continue to penetrate and create their own vision of the piece. Not only does Busoni provide plenty of *ossia* passages, but he also provides choices for the performer (such as the option to include all thirty variations if desired, and the choice to use either Variation 14 or Variation 17). For such an important work by a major composer, this editing approach was highly unusual. For the Goldberg Variations, it was unprecedented.

Busoni believed that some of the variations were unnecessary, and in the preface to his published edition he suggested that performers eliminate nine of the variations as he did in his own performances, stating "I considered it expedient, for public performance, to suppress entirely some of the Variations."[38] However, he included all of the

---

38. Busoni, preface to *Aria mit 30 Veränderungen*, 3.

variations in his published edition, in case performers still wanted to play them. For instance, he suggested eliminating Variation 3, the canon at the unison, because he felt that its character was already expressed in Variation 2. This then places greater weight on the fast-paced virtuoso variations and reduces the total length of the piece (placing it at about the length of an average Beethoven sonata), something Busoni might have been keen on as a performer. In addition, he suggested eliminating several variations that would obscure a tripartite structure. For instance, he disliked the Overture (Variation 16), which he stated broke the momentum. Busoni considered Variation 25 to be the culminating point and the most profound variation. He argued that all that followed should be a "winding-up." Thus he wanted to eliminate the canon at the ninth (Variation 27), which he thought impeded the movement to the end.[39]

In addition to modifying the form of the piece, Busoni also transcribed it for piano. In this he followed in the tradition of many of the editors in the generation immediately preceding him, such as Czerny. In terms of notation, Busoni wrote out most of the ornaments, added rests and ties, and clarified the voicing. He also re-notated pitches to keep the same voices on the same staff.

Yet, even in his notational choices, Busoni sought to blend his voice with Bach's. Busoni's numerous performance suggestions were designed to fully exploit the expressive capabilities of the piano while still imitating the textural and coloristic possibilities of the harpsichord—an instrument he knew very well, as he owned a Dolmetsch harpsichord (see Figure 3.2).[40] He added affective markings throughout (such as "Largamente e cantato" for the Aria and "Allegro con freschezza, e deciso. Frisch." for Variation 1). In Variation 1, measures 13–14, he changed the register to eliminate the awkwardness of the hand crossings on a single manual. In some cases, he used three staves (as in Variation 15) to explicate hand crossings on a one-manual piano. In addition, he removed any arpeggiated chords that are necessary on the harpsichord for their sustaining value but not needed on the piano, as in Variation 16.

Nonetheless, he hoped to retain the coloristic and textural variety possible on many harpsichords. He added numerous slurs and articulation marks, many suggesting an overall detached and clearly articulated touch (in stark contrast to Czerny's overall legato approach). For Variation 3, he suggested emulating trio sonata texture with different instruments (*quasi oboe, quasi flauto*) on three staves—a texture more easily imitated on some harpsichords. In Variation 24, he notes that lines could be played as if on a clarinet and bassoon. In Variation 2, he doubled octaves in the bass throughout to create a richer sound.

39. Ibid., 4.

40. Arnold Dolmetsch introduced Busoni to the harpsichord in 1910 and later built an instrument for him. Busoni's instrument is now owned by Yale University.

FERRUCCIO BUSONI
AT THE HARPSICHORD

Figure 3.2. Busoni playing the harpsichord. Photographer unknown, courtesy Boston Symphony Orchestra Archives.

At the same time, some of his suggestions were structural, and this again is a departure from the other editors who preceded him. In some cases, he provided additional lines to enrich the texture, such as the extra counterpoint in Variation 1 in measures 25–26 (see m. 25 in Example 3.3). In Variation 5, he created two lines out of the right-hand figural work in measure 6 and offered alternative passages that he believed "improved upon" Bach's writing. In Variation 8, he suggested holding down the first note in the left hand—something not possible on the harpsichord but quite effective on the piano. In other cases, he again added to the texture and complexity by inserting additional lines (as in Variation 13, when he added an inner voice in mm. 21–23) and ornamentation (as in the treble in Variation 11, mm. 30–31). He added a new melody in Variation 13 and repeated notes in Variation 20 (see Examples 3.4 and 3.5).

Reception

The initial reception of Busoni's Goldberg Variations was predominantly positive. Audiences in Berlin, as discussed above, were appreciative of Busoni's attempts to make the piece more accessible. Isidor Philipp, to whom the edition is dedicated, called it "magnificent" and implied he would perform and teach only Busoni's Goldberg

Example 3.3. Busoni's Goldberg
Variations, Variation 1, m. 25.

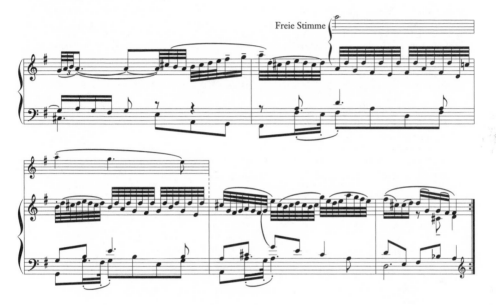

Example 3.4. Busoni's Goldberg Variations, Variation 13, mm. 12–16.

Example 3.5. Busoni's Goldberg Variations, Variation 20, mm. 1–2.

Variations in the future.[41] Busoni also proudly noted in 1917 that his edition had been made widely accessible in a four-language edition (German, English, French, Italian), suggesting its commercial value and widespread acceptance.[42]

After his death, Busoni's arrangement of the Goldberg Variations was performed by a few of his students.[43] Two of Busoni's best-known pupils, Egon Petri and Erwin Bodky, performed the Goldberg Variations in the 1920s and 1930s. Petri used the Busoni arrangement in New York in the 1930s, but little is known about his interpretation, as no recordings seem to exist. One reviewer praised his renditions of music by Liszt and of Busoni's Sonatina No. 6, BV 284, while criticizing his performance of Bach as cold: "Although he did much expert playing in the Bach Variations, of which he omitted ten out of the thirty, his was a rather cold and rushed interpretation of this masterpiece, which has much more to say than he expounded."[44] Earl Wild, a pupil of Petri's, on the other hand, had quite a different reaction to his Bach interpretations, describing them as exquisite.[45] Bodky also performed the Busoni version of the Goldberg Variations on the piano in Germany, including at his first professional recital in Berlin in 1920. He later performed it on harpsichord, such as in the Netherlands in 1933, when he also played Beethoven's "Hammerklavier Sonata" on piano.[46]

The Goldberg Variations, while a rarity in Busoni's lifetime, eventually became a major part of the repertoire. James Friskin was probably the first to perform the entire Goldberg Variations in the United States, doing so in 1925 on piano.[47] Wanda Landowska recorded it for the first time on her modern harpsichord in 1933 and was

41. Isidor Philipp, "Speaking for Busoni," *New York Times*, 8 March 1942.

42. Busoni, letter of 21 March 1917 to José Vianna da Motta, in *Ferruccio Busoni: Selected Letters*, 255.

43. For a more comprehensive overview of the reception of the Goldberg Variations, see Peter Williams, *Bach: The Goldberg Variations*, Cambridge Music Handbooks (Cambridge: Cambridge University Press, 2001).

44. "Egon Petri Gives Recital of Liszt," *New York Times*, 16 February 1936.

45. Earl Wild, *A Walk on the Wild Side: A Memoir by Virtuoso Pianist Earl Wild* (Palm Springs, Calif.: Ivory Classics Foundation, 2011). Wild studied with Petri in New York for about one year (1934), 89. Petri passed down the Busoni "Goldberg" tradition to other students as well. Paul Doguereau, for instance, who studied for three years with Petri in Zakopane, studied the Goldberg Variations with him. See Lesley A. Wright, *Perspectives on the Performance of French Piano Music* (Burlington, Vt.: Ashgate, 2014).

46. Mark Lindley, "Erwin Bodky (1896–1958), a Prussian in Boston," *Jahrbuch des Staatlichen Instituts für Musikforschung Preußischer Kulturbesitz*, 2011, 229–42.

47. "Mr. Friskin played them from beginning to end without faltering, with a smooth and flowing technic and a delicate appreciation of their dexterity. He communicated his genuine delight in this work of art to his listeners, who applauded the pianist for bringing this great composition from its comparative obscurity." "Friskin Gives a Novelty: Pianist Plays All of the Goldberg Variations of Bach," *New York Times*, 19 March 1925. See also the following for reactions to the performance: Sylvanus

followed soon after by Rosalyn Tureck and Jörg Demus on piano. Glenn Gould's famous piano recording was not produced until 1955, when interpretations on harpsichord were most prevalent.[48] After Gould, the piece became a staple on the piano. Just a few pianists to program the piece include Rudolf Serkin, Philip Lévi, Eduard Erdmann, Claudio Arrau, and Wilhelm Backhaus.

Yet with the rise of the early music movement with its emphasis on historically informed performance practice, it became unpopular to perform Busoni's Goldberg Variations. Despite the prevalence of the Goldberg Variations in the repertoire of harpsichordists and pianists beginning in the 1930s, it would not be until the 1990s that another performance of the Bach-Busoni Goldberg Variations would take place. Six more recordings followed in rapid succession (see Table 3.3). Four performers chose to follow Busoni's suggestion to cut nine of the variations, and three chose to substitute Variation 14 with Variation 17. They treated Busoni's arrangement as a "work" to be followed fairly precisely, even despite their unique interpretive approaches. Where they differed most from one another and from Busoni's score was in terms of tempo, dynamics, and articulation. Sara Davis (David) Buechner's performance was richly expressive and lyrical, with rubato and long pauses between the three "movements." Buechner also created short sets in some cases, by starting variations at the dynamic level and tempo of the previous ones. Claudius Tanski, on the other hand, displayed stark contrasts in tempo and dynamics between variations. He played with a detached touch overall and with resultant clarity.[49] Izumi Amano's recording was from a live recital at the Wako University in Tokyo, Japan.[50] One distinctive characteristic of

Urban, "Goldberg's Bach Variations," *New York Times*, 22 March 1925; and Winthrop Parkhurst, "Bach's *Goldberg Variations* Again," *New York Times*, 29 March 1925.

48. Jonathan Summers, liner notes to Glenn Gould, *Bach: Goldberg Variations*, BWV 988, recorded June 1955, Naxos Historical 8.111247, 2007, compact disc; text accessed 25 July 2017, https://www.chandos.net/chanimages/Booklets/NH1247.pdf.

49. Claudius Tanski, *Bach/Busoni, Goldberg Variations*, recorded 15–16 July 2004, MDG 312 1323–2, 2005, compact disc. Tanski's most important teacher was Alfred Brendel, and he has received numerous awards and international prizes (Vercelli, Bolzano, and Budapest among others). He is a solo and a chamber musician and has taught at the Mozarteum University in Salzburg since 1988. He has created radio or television portraits of Ferruccio Busoni, Julius Reubke, and Felix Draeseke. David Buechner, *Bach-Busoni "Goldberg Variations": World Premiere Recording*, recorded 3–5 September 1995, Connoisseur Society 4212, 1996, compact disc. Buechner was a prizewinner in many major international competitions, including Queen Elisabeth (Brussels), Leeds, Mozart (Salzburg), Beethoven (Vienna), and Sydney. Buechner has taught at the Manhattan School of Music, New York University, and the University of British Columbia and joined the faculty of Temple University's Boyer College of Music and Dance in 2016.

50. Izumi Amano, piano, "Goldberg Variations," by J. S. Bach, arr. Busoni, recorded live on 25 December 2015, accessed 3 August 2017, https://www.youtube.com/watch?v=ibmpMsQzR-I.

Table 3.3. Recordings of the Bach-Busoni Goldberg Variations

1996, David Buechner (Sara Davis Buechner), Busoni arrangement
2004, Claudius Tanski, Busoni arrangement
2009, Ming Aldrich-Gan, Busoni edition—all 30 variations
2014, Tzimon Barto, Busoni edition—all 30 variations
2015, Izumi Amano, Busoni arrangement
2017 and 2018, Chiara Bertoglio, Busoni arrangement
2019, Chiyan Wong, Busoni edition—all 30 variations

Note: Each date listed represents the date the piece was recorded, not the recording release date.

her performance is the use of nearly constant pedal throughout. Chiara Bertoglio's approach is remarkable for its clarity of touch and for its dramatic approach to the ending. Bertoglio unabashedly concludes with *forte* and bold octaves in the final aria.

Chiyan Wong, a rising pianist and noted Busoni interpreter, also chose to follow Busoni's suggested structure for the piece but decided to retain Variation 14.[51] He has recently performed Busoni's version of the Goldberg Variations in his 2017–18 programs to great acclaim. When asked why he chose this version, he wrote that he was fascinated by Busoni's interest in Bach's musical genealogy and how interpretations have evolved over time. In addition, he states that he now "think[s] of the music very much in Busoni's [tripartite] structure."[52] He has indicated, however, that he was interested in choosing elements from Busoni's version as well as from Bach's original.

Wong's approach is like a musical dialogue between the Bach original, the Busoni arrangement, and his own ideas. He chose not to play Busoni's bombastic version of the Aria at the end of the piece. In addition, he inserted some of his own ideas about ornamentation, including in the opening aria, where he more closely adhered to the notation in the Ralph Kirkpatrick edition and omitted the octave doublings in the bass during the final bars (except during the da capo). In addition, he made numerous small alterations to the text, including the following:

> Variation 2—used Bach's (rather than Busoni's) pattern in the bass.
> Variation 4—played the B octave in the bass as a semiquaver (m. 31).
> Variation 5—omitted Busoni's octaves in measures 4–7.
> Variation 8—relied on Bach's original in measures 16 and 32, with the left-hand passage an octave higher.
> Variation 10—played *spiccatissimo* instead of *tenuto*, and not *quasi f*, but *mezzo p*.

51. Private recordings have been made of Wong's live performances of the Goldberg Variations. Wong, e-mail message to author, 16 April 2019.

52. Chiyan Wong, e-mail messages to author, 25 July and 20 October 2017. Wong is a graduate of the Royal Academy of Music. He is a recipient of numerous awards and performs internationally.

Variation 14—performed this variation instead of Variation 17.

Variation 15—chose not to observe the trills and register changes as notated in the Busoni version.

Variation 26—changed pitches (last sextuplet group in left hand is played: A, G, F-sharp, E, F-sharp, D-sharp).[53]

By contrast, two other performers chose to disregard Busoni's suggestions for abbreviating the piece, choosing instead to play all thirty variations. One of these performers, Ming Aldrich-Gan, studied at Bard College with Peter Serkin, whose father, Rudolf Serkin, had met Busoni.[54] Aldrich-Gan stated that it was no longer necessary to shorten the piece, because audiences were used to listening to the entire work. He wrote that his recording might not reflect all of Busoni's notated ideas but that it would be in line with the Busonian spirit of continuous innovation: "I also did take quite a few liberties of my own. In any case, I'm sure that my interpretation will be as controversial as Busoni's edition itself—but in the end, I believe very strongly in the freedom of interpretation of each individual performer, and that the evolution of a piece does not stop at the death of the composer."[55] What he most valued in Busoni's arrangement was the way he made the piece pianistic.[56] Ming's own additions are numerous. Contrary to Busoni's edition, he often slightly displaces the left and right hands, including in the opening aria. He adds ornamentation throughout as well, including in Variation 2, which he plays in a very detached manner, and in the soprano part in the second half of Variation 3. He also groups variations together, such as when he starts Variations 4 and 7 without a pause. He also adds even more octaves than Busoni, putting them at the conclusion of Variations 7 and 9, as well as throughout Variation 10.[57]

Tzimon Barto, who likewise recorded all thirty variations, had played through them several times from the Henle edition but did not feel really drawn to the piece until

53. Ibid.

54. The Serkins have a direct connection to Busoni. Rudolph Serkin wrote to Busoni, asking to be his student, but he never responded. However, in May and December 1921 he heard Busoni perform his adaptations of the last twelve Mozart concertos in Berlin. Serkin and Adolf Busch learned Busoni's second violin sonata and gained an audience with Busoni, who listened to them. However, Busoni said that Serkin was too old to study with him. He reportedly told Serkin to attend many concerts and to play with more pedal.

55. Ming Aldrich-Gan, "Bach/Busoni Concerto and Goldberg Variations," *Piano Society Forum*, 10 December 2009, accessed 30 July 2017, http://www.pianosociety.com/threads/forum-exclusive-bach -busoni-concerto-goldberg-variati.3917/.

56. Ming Aldrich-Gan, *Bach (Busonified): Concerto in D Minor; Goldberg Variations*, liner notes, Cdbaby 2009, accessed 30 July 2017, https://store.cdbaby.com/cd/MingAldrichGan.

57. Ming Aldrich-Gan, *Bach (Busonified): Concerto in D Minor; Goldberg Variations*, accessed 17 July 2017, https://www.youtube.com/watch?v=bI4pFyEx3xc.

he tried out Busoni's version.[58] He loved Busoni's addition of octaves, his approach to phrasing, and his ornamentation.[59] Yet he decided not to follow Busoni's directions for the ending, choosing instead to reprise the Aria as originally written and to bypass Busoni's alterations of Variations 29 and 30. He stated that he could not imagine playing the final Aria *forte* and with such power; it went against his conception of the aria.[60] He also decided not to add the jazzy repeated notes suggested by Busoni for Variation 20.

Barto often performs from scores in which he writes out his own ideas too; he believes it is really up to the interpreter to discover what the notation means and to play as he or she is inspired. However, Barto's disregard for traditions about playing Bach is evident from his recording, which could be called the Bach-Busoni-Barto version of the Goldberg Variations. Although he chooses to follow aspects of Busoni's arrangement, he simultaneously exerts his own distinctive interpretive stamp, characterized by his lyrical shaping of phrases. Barto's interpretation thus does not resemble the bold and intellectual approach reportedly characteristic of Busoni's piano playing. Barto adds a sentimental romantic spirit with frequent *crescendos, diminuendos, ritardandos,* and *accelerandos.* He crafts and shapes each phrase and each voice like a singer would, and with as many dynamic gradations as possible.[61]

Conclusion

Busoni's Goldberg Variations offered some ideas about how the piece could be realized on the piano. At the same time it provided several options for ways Bach's music could be modified for the concert hall in an age in which the piece was hardly known. Yet Busoni's suggested modifications went beyond what most others were doing with the piece during and immediately after his lifetime. The burgeoning early music movement with its search for authentic sounds on historical instruments that was already developing by the end of the nineteenth century, coupled with the rise of the concept

58. Tzimon Barto, e-mail message to author, 5 August 2017.

59. Tzimon Barto, *Bach Goldberg Variations*, recorded 13–14 May 2014, Capriccio C5243, 2015, compact disc. Barto studied at the Juilliard School with Adele Marcus and won the Gina Bachauer Competition two years in succession. He has recorded extensively and performed internationally. As an author and a pianist, he seeks to combine poetry and music. His unconventional interpretations generally elicit praise in Germany and disdain in England. See Anne Midgette, "Tzimon Barto: An Unconventional Pianist, Philosopher, Reformed Drug Addict," *Washington Post*, 16 January 2011.

60. Barto, e-mail message to author, 5 August 2017.

61. For a review of Barto's recording, see Rune Naljoss, "Not Your Grandmother's Goldberg Variations" (23 July 2017), accessed 31 July 2017, https://www.amazon.com/Bach-Goldberg-Variations-Tzimon-Barto/dp/B00U0S0NDG.

of *Werktreue*, promoted historically informed performances that sought to recreate the notated text more literally.

The disappearance of Busoni's Goldberg Variations from the concert halls is thus not as surprising as the version's resurrection in the twenty-first century. Six different people made recordings of it in the first two decades of the twenty-first century alone. This sudden interest in Busoni's version of the Goldberg Variations is not an aberration. The revival of interest in it correlates with a dramatic increase in the number of new arrangements of the Goldberg Variations (notated or recorded or both) in the twenty-first century in general. The first two decades of the century yielded roughly two times the number of arrangements as in the previous two centuries put together (thirty-two arrangements plus five multiple-author reworkings in the twenty-first century versus sixteen arrangements and one multiple-author reworking in the previous two centuries) (see Tables 3.4 and 3.5). Part of the increase could be attributed to the prevalence of recording equipment today. Yet the dearth of reworkings between the years 1938 and 1975—at the height of the authenticity movement, and precisely when Busoni's version was shunned as well—is noteworthy.

The recent interest in Busoni's Goldberg Variations thus appears to be part of a larger trend in performance ideals, characterized by a less rigid approach toward the score and the composer's intent. Richard Taruskin has argued that the *Werktreue* movement was, in fact, mainly a reflection of twentieth-century ideals. His prediction was that an idealization of textual fidelity and related values would wane with the decline of modernism:

> The ideal of authentistic performance grew up alongside modernism, shares its tenets, and will probably decline alongside it as well. Its values, its justification, and, yes, its authenticity will only be revealed in conjunction with those of modernism. Historical verisimilitude, composers' intentions, original instruments, and all that, to the extent that they have a bearing on the question, have not been ends but means; and in most considerations of the issue they have been smoke screens. To put my thesis in a nutshell, I hold that "historical" performance today is not really historical; that a specious veneer of historicism clothes a performance style that is completely of our own time, and is in fact the most modern style around.[62]

Indeed, a growing number of performers today exhibit a preference for deconstructionist or postmodernist approaches. They are decidedly against firm traditions and rules; they still respect a composer's notated ideas but do not consider them complete. In an age of postmodernism, globalization, and deconstructionism—trends that are anti-positivistic and focused on the breaking down of divisions, barriers, and walls,

62. Richard Taruskin, *Text and Act: Essays on Music and Performance* (New York: Oxford University Press, 1995), 102.

Table 3.4. Arrangements of the Goldberg Variations

1840s, Carl Czerny

1870, Sir Francis Tovey, solo piano

1883, Josef Rheinberger, two pianos

1902, Karl Klindworth, solo piano[a]

1912, Karl Eichler, piano duet (four hands)

1915, Ferruccio Busoni, solo piano

1915, Josef Rheinberger and Max Reger, two pianos

1926, Wilhelm Middelschulte, organ[b]

1933, Gino Tagliapietra, solo piano

1938, Józef Koffler, small orchestra/string orchestra

1975, Charles Ramirez and Helen Kalamuniak, two guitars

1984, Dmitry Sitkovetsky, string trio

1986, John and Mirjana Lewis, harpsichord and piano

1987, Jean Guillou, organ

1988, Joel Spiegelman, synthesizer

1997, József Eötvös, guitar

2000, Uri Caine, large instrumental ensemble (historical, classical, and jazz)

2000, Jacques Loussier, jazz trio

2001, Wolfgang Dimetrik, accordion

2001, Kálmán Oláh, jazz piano and bass

2002, Robin Holloway, two pianos

2002, Veronica Kraneis, flute, viola, and cello

2003, Marcel Bitsch, octet

2003, Karlheinz Essl, string trio and live electronics

2003, Francesco Venerucci, saxophone quartet

2004, Mika Väyrynen, accordion

2006, Pius Cheung, marimba

2006, Andrei Eshpai, woodwind ensemble

2006, Sax Allemande, saxophone trio or quartet

2007, Sebastian Gramms, bass, tenor saxophone, trombone, guitar, and drums

2008, Teodoro Anzellotti, accordion

2008, Richard Crowell, harp, cello, oboe, flute, and more

2008, Daniel Sullivan, organ

2008, Eva Tamassy, flute and harpsichord or organ

2008, Stephen Thorneycroft and Stephen Tafra, two classical guitars

2009, Andreas Almqvist, guitar

2009, Sylvain Blassel, harp

2009, Jeremiah Bornfield, keyboard

2009, Catrin Finch, harp

2009, Silke Strauf and Claas Harders, two viols

2010, Federico Sarudiansky, string trio

2011, Richard Boothby, viols

2011, Andy Fite, jazz guitar

2013, Dan Tepfer, solo piano
2014, Steve Shorter, guitar ensemble
2015, Scottish Ensemble and Andersson Dance, string orchestra and five dancers
2016, Mika Pohjola, piano, harpsichord, and string quartet
2016, Simon Proulx, acoustic mandolin, baritone guitar

Note: This list includes editions intentionally adapted for solo piano, transcriptions for other instruments, and arrangements either recorded or published in printed form.

[a] "The composer wrote these wonderful variations known as the 'Goldberg' for a harpsichord with two keyboards; such an instrument at the present day is, however, rare, so that this clever transcription for pianoforte will be welcome." "Karl Klindworth," *The Athenaeum*, 30 August 1902, 294.

[b] Jürgen Sonnentheil, "Master of Counterpoint: Wilhelm Middelschulte and His Arrangement of the Goldberg Variations for Organ," *Organ: Journal für die Orgel* 5.1 (2002): 44–53.

Table 3.5. Multiple-Author Adaptations of the Goldberg Variations

1997, The New Goldberg Variations
2004, 13 Ways of Looking at the Goldberg
2004, bODY_rEMIX/gOLDBERG_vARIATIONS
2007, Goldberg's Ghost
2008, Bufo Variations
2013–2016, Goldberg Werk

including divisions between composer and interpreter—many performers see themselves as playing a more active role in discovering information that is not clear from or that cannot be conveyed by notation. Bruce Haynes has noted that the "cover band mentality," as he calls it, and period composing are on the rise.[63] Barto, for instance, has articulated skepticism about striving to recreate a composer's original intentions: "'I don't get this, "You have to do what the composer wanted,"'" he says, cheerfully uttering a classical-music heresy. 'We're living in a deconstructionist age.' He doesn't think an unusual interpretation can damage a masterpiece."[64] Aldrich-Gan also stated that compositions are not completed when notated by the composer and that interpreters have the right to change things when performing: "I believe very strongly in the freedom of interpretation of each individual performer, and that the evolution of a piece does not stop at the death of the composer."[65] These attitudes seem to echo Busoni's.

63. Bruce Haynes, *The End of Early Music: A Period Performer's History of Music for the Twenty-First Century* (New York: Oxford University Press, 2007), 203–27.

64. Midgette, "Tzimon Barto: An Unconventional Pianist."

65. Aldrich-Gan, "Bach/Busoni Concerto and Goldberg Variations."

Rosen's criticisms of Busoni's Goldberg Variations for going beyond the score are thus becoming as much a symbol of a passing era as Busoni's freedom with the text was of late romanticism. While most performers today have some reservations about modifying Bach to the degree that Busoni did, many like to have choices, and Busoni's version contained good ideas about how to play Bach's harpsichord music on the piano, even if it went too far—in the estimation of some. Now performers can choose between what Bach notated, what Busoni modified, and what they want to play. For some, it is no longer about the quest for a "correct" or "authentic" recreation of a text, or of a composer's wishes, or of a quest for audience applause, but of a notion of musical possibilities and a collaboration of ideas separated by centuries but united by an exploration of a common text. It is about playing as one wants to play, as Barto puts it, such that the notes resound anew with previously unimagined possibilities.[66] And this is precisely what Busoni had hoped would happen when he created his own open edition of the Goldberg Variations.

66. Barto, e-mail message to author, 5 August 2017.

Bach as Modern Jazz

Stephen A. Crist

E ver since Eddie South, Stéphane Grappelli, and Django Reinhardt recorded the Concerto in D Minor for Two Violins, BWV 1043, in 1937, jazz musicians have either engaged with J. S. Bach's music directly or felt his influence indirectly. For instance, in connection with the Bach tercentenary, the great jazz pianist Oscar Peterson composed and recorded the three-movement *Bach Suite* (1985).[1] Moreover, Bach festivals in Germany and elsewhere frequently include jazz concerts. The 2018 Bachfest in Leipzig, for example, featured Stephan König's jazz arrangement of Bach's *Christmas Oratorio*. Such projects are legion, and they show no signs of abating. Another recent case in point is *After Bach*, a new album in which the American jazz pianist Brad Mehldau plays several pieces from *The Well-Tempered Clavier*, interspersed with his own "After Bach" (and "Before Bach") compositions.[2]

Yet there has been very little investigation of the Bach-inspired jazz repertoire, despite its depth and breadth. A substantial article on the recordings of BWV 1043 mentioned above appeared in 2006.[3] A few years earlier, I published a chapter about Bach's influence on Dave Brubeck.[4] But there are surprisingly few other such writings, and research on "Bach and jazz" remains largely uncharted territory.[5]

---

1. *Oscar Peterson Live*, Pablo PACD-2310–940–2, 1990, compact disc. According to Peterson's own testimony in the liner notes by Leonard Feather, he created the suite on a commission from the Montreal Bach Festival.

2. Brad Mehldau, *After Bach*, Nonesuch 755979 31880, 2018, compact disc.

3. Benjamin Givan, "The South-Grappelli Recordings of the Bach *Double Violin Concerto*," *Popular Music and Society* 29 (2006): 335–57.

4. Stephen A. Crist, "The Role and Meaning of the Bach Chorale in the Music of Dave Brubeck," in *Bach in America*, ed. Stephen A. Crist, Bach Perspectives 5 (Urbana: University of Illinois Press, 2003), 179–215. This essay examines Brubeck's oratorios and other works in the "classical" mold as well as his jazz.

5. A broad survey, encompassing rock music as well as jazz, is found in Bernward Halbscheffel, "Bach und Jazz und Rock," in *Johann Sebastian Bach und die Gegenwart: Beiträge zur Bach-Rezeption, 1945–2005*, ed. Michael Heinemann and Hans-Joachim Hinrichsen (Cologne: Dohr, 2007), 59–105.

Among the many tributes to Bach by jazz musicians over the years, the 1974 *Blues on Bach* album by the Modern Jazz Quartet is one of the most important. This is because the MJQ, as it came to be known, was a leading jazz combo of its era—beginning in the early 1950s and continuing through 1974, with several subsequent reunions in the 1980s and early 1990s. The group was artistically and commercially quite successful, routinely placing high on both the critics' and readers' polls of jazz publications such as *Down Beat* magazine. The MJQ swam in the same waters, so to speak, as the ensembles of major jazz figures such as Duke Ellington, Miles Davis, Dave Brubeck, and Ornette Coleman. In other words, it was a regular jazz unit—unlike, say, the Jacques Loussier Trio or the Swingle Singers, both of which specialized in "jazzy" performances of Bach's music. *Blues on Bach* was the MJQ's last studio album before the quartet disbanded. It represents the culmination of this particular strand of the group's creative output, and it forms the centerpiece of my study. But the album was preceded by more than two decades of preparatory work. Accordingly, I will discuss a pair of recordings from the MJQ's early years before examining *Blues on Bach*. And I will conclude with a brief consideration of a related project from the 1980s, John Lewis's renditions of all twenty-four preludes and fugues from Book 1 of *The Well-Tempered Clavier*.

"Vendome"

Though some of its members had performed together in the 1940s as the rhythm section of the Dizzy Gillespie Orchestra, the Modern Jazz Quartet began playing under that name in 1952. During the last few days of that year, the four musicians recorded four tunes that constituted the A side of their first LP, which was released the next year on the Prestige label.[6] The third cut, titled "Vendome" (after the famous Place Vendôme in Paris), is an original composition by the combo's pianist and music director, John Lewis, along with Milt Jackson on vibraphone, Percy Heath on bass, and Kenny Clarke on drums. Though clearly in the jazz idiom, it begins with a fugal exposition (see Example 4.1). The subject is played on the vibraphone at the

---

In the present context, it is worth mentioning as well a pioneering study that was published as Hans-Peter Schmitz, "Baroque Music and Jazz," trans. Dominique-René de Lerma, *The Black Perspective in Music* 7 (1979): 75–80. Schmitz's article, which is not focused specifically on Bach (and also not entirely successful), attempted to draw broad parallels between performance practices in these two divergent repertoires. It originally appeared shortly after World War II in *Stimmen*, the erstwhile publication of the German chapter of the Internationale Gesellschaft für Neue Musik ("Jazz und Alte Musik," *Stimmen: Monatsblätter für Musik* 18 [1949]: 497–500), and was reprinted in *Tibia: Magazin für Holzbläser* 23 (1998): 257–61.

6. *The Modern Jazz Quartet*, Prestige PRLP 160, 1953, 33⅓ rpm. The A side was recorded on 22 December 1952 and the B side (four additional tracks) on 25 June 1953.

Example 4.1. "Vendome," fugal exposition (mm. 1–13).

beginning, then repeated at the upper octave (mm. 6–9). Meanwhile, the answer is heard first in the right hand of the piano (mm. 3–6), then in the left hand (mm. 9–12), and the bass serves an accompanimental function, more or less in the role of a basso continuo.

Comparison of the differing forms of the subject and answer in "Vendome" reveals that Lewis's approach to fugal procedure was more relaxed than generally is the case with Bach. The presence of a bass line also differentiates this jazz fugue from its baroque models. The subsequent course of this short piece (just over three minutes) involves alternation between expositions and episodes. There are three sets of expositions and episodes, and the movement is rounded off with a brief stretto passage (beginning at 2:47). In addition to the other differences between composed expositions and improvised episodes, the eighth notes are played in straight rhythm in the former, and they are swung in the latter.[7]

"Softly, as in a Morning Sunrise"

"Vendome" is just one of John Lewis's fugal compositions from the early years of the MJQ. Others include "Concorde" (1955), "Versailles" (1956), "A Fugue for Music Inn" (1956), and "Three Windows" (1957).[8] "Concorde" was the title track of the MJQ's 1955 LP, which also contained the group's version of the standard "Softly, as in a Morning Sunrise."[9] This song, with music by Sigmund Romberg and lyrics by Oscar Hammerstein II, originated in the operetta *The New Moon* (1928), but it has been arranged and recorded by countless jazz musicians over the course of its ninety-year history.

In the MJQ version, an embellished form of the melody is played by Milt Jackson on the vibraphone (Example 4.2).[10] The eight-bar introduction has a rather distinguished pedigree: it is the canon *a 2 Violini in unisono* from Bach's *Musical Offering*, BWV 1079, with the bass playing the Royal Theme (Example 4.3). Similarly, the outro is a truncated version of the same canon.

---

7. A serviceable analytical diagram of "Vendome" and accompanying discussion are found in Wolfram Knauer, *Zwischen Bebop und Free Jazz: Komposition und Improvisation des Modern Jazz Quartet* (Mainz: Schott, 1990), 1:125–26. This study also includes a comparative analysis of four MJQ performances of "Vendome." See 1:225–33, and synoptic transcriptions from the recordings in 2:125–44. According to Knauer, Lewis said in a 1984 interview that he composed "Vendome" as a composition exercise during his studies at the Manhattan School of Music (1:225).

8. See ibid., 1:120–39.

9. The Modern Jazz Quartet, *Concorde*, Prestige PRLP 7005, 1955, 33⅓ rpm.

10. The group's drummer at this point was Connie Kay, who in 1955 had just replaced Kenny Clarke. Kay remained a member of the MJQ until his death in 1994.

Example 4.2. "Softly, as in a Morning Sunrise," first phrase of melody (mm. 9–15).

Example 4.3. "Softly, as in a Morning Sunrise," introduction (mm. 1–8).

There is no documentary evidence concerning how or where Lewis came into contact with the *Musical Offering* and decided to incorporate this canon into his arrangement. It seems likely, however, that it was sometime after April 1952, when he first recorded "Softly, as in a Morning Sunrise" with a group known as "Milt Jackson's Quartet" (the original MJQ, with Percy Heath on bass and Kenny Clarke on drums).[11] His introduction on the earlier recording is a surprisingly flat-footed chord progression, just four bars in length.

11. Hi-Lo 1412, 1952, 78 rpm. Rereleased on *The Quartet*, Savoy MG-12046, 1956, 33⅓ rpm.

It may be that Lewis was exposed to the *Musical Offering* while studying for the master's degree he earned from the Manhattan School of Music in 1953. But whether he became familiar with this work as part of his curriculum or in some other context, what seems to have caught Lewis's ear was the motivic connection between the first two notes of the Romberg and Hammerstein song—a descending fourth from the tonic to the dominant—and the first two notes of Bach's canon, which also form a descending interval, but from 5 to 1, instead of the opposite.

In terms of Bachian influence on these early MJQ arrangements, then, "Vendome" represents the general (a newly composed but Bach-like fugue), while "Softly, as in a Morning Sunrise" represents the specific (a literal quotation from a particular, identifiable work by Bach).

The Blues in *Blues on Bach*

One of the Modern Jazz Quartet's most significant claims to fame is that the members remained intact as a group for more than twenty years—even longer than the Dave Brubeck Quartet, which frequently is touted as a paragon of longevity among jazz combos.[12] The MJQ signed with Atlantic Records and issued an extensive and distinguished series of albums from 1956 until 1974, when its members went their separate ways (until their subsequent reunions). "Vendome," "Softly, as in a Morning Sunrise," and many other compositions and arrangements with connections to Bach and other classical composers were a standard part of the group's repertoire, both in live performance and in the studio.[13]

The MJQ's last studio album for Atlantic was a tribute to J. S. Bach titled *Blues on Bach*.[14] It consists of nine cuts, which alternate between two different concepts. John Lewis's arrangements of compositions by Bach (or attributed to him) will be examined in the next section. The even-numbered tracks (2 and 4 on side 1, and 2 and 4 on side 2) make up a series of blues originals, in the keys of B-flat major, A minor, C minor, and B major—a set of tonalities that spells out Bach's name in the German pitch nomenclature. These four tunes were recorded in New York City on the Tuesday after Thanksgiving (November 27) in 1973, and they are the meat of the album, in both

12. The "classic" Dave Brubeck Quartet—with Brubeck on piano, Paul Desmond on alto saxophone, Joe Morello on drums (from 1956), and Eugene Wright on bass (from 1958)—was active for sixteen years, from 1951 until 1967.

13. In addition to the pieces mentioned already, other key works include "The Queen's Fancy" on *The Modern Jazz Quartet with Milt Jackson*, Prestige PRLP 160, 1953, 33⅓ rpm; "Fugato" on The Modern Jazz Quartet, *Lonely Woman*, Atlantic 1381, 1962, 33⅓ rpm; and "Pulcinella" and "Piazza Navona" from The Modern Jazz Quartet, *The Comedy*, Atlantic 1390, 1962, 33⅓ rpm.

14. The Modern Jazz Quartet, *Blues on Bach*, Atlantic 1652, 1974, 33⅓ rpm.

quantity and quality. They account for nearly two-thirds of the album's total playing time, and the level of performance is very high. The MJQ was especially famous for its blues, so these cuts represent the work of seasoned blues masters at the top of their game. They confirm the opinion of the eminent jazz critic Gary Giddins, who averred that "no contemporary band was more devoted to or as enterprising in exploring and sustaining the worldly elegance of the blues."[15]

This is not the place for exhaustive analysis of all four blues numbers on *Blues on Bach*, because this music has little to do with Bach in any direct way (it contains no embedded motives, for instance). What these tunes do illustrate, however, is that the MJQ was profoundly committed to the pursuit of maximum diversity within this genre. Just as the individual chorale preludes in the *Orgelbüchlein*, or the six items that make up the *Brandenburg Concertos*—or, indeed, the constituent parts of any collection of works by Bach—exhibit the composer's commitment to systematic exploration of the inherent possibilities of particular musical forms and procedures, so we encounter here a multiplicity of approaches to the standard format of the blues, a quintessential pattern in jazz.

The prototypical twelve-bar blues consists of three four-bar segments, with the following harmonic progression:

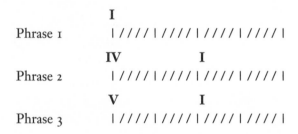

Against this backdrop, Lewis's "Blues in B Flat" stands out in several respects. Most importantly, it departs from the usual sequence of chords by beginning with the subdominant instead of the tonic. The second phrase then proceeds to four bars of tonic, and the third phrase moves nearly as usual from V to IV (one bar each) to I (two bars). This pattern is further complicated by appending four additional bars of the subdominant at the beginning (in other words, the first strain extends to sixteen bars instead of twelve, and the first eight are in the subdominant). Another peculiarity of the head is its jaunty chromatic motion, moving repeatedly from an E-flat major chord to E-natural and back, and similarly between B-flat major and B-natural. The principal soloist is the vibraphonist Milt Jackson, who takes four twelve-bar choruses

15. Gary Giddins, "Modern Jazz Quartet (the First Forty Years)," in *Visions of Jazz: The First Century* (New York: Oxford University Press, 1998), 388.

that display his prodigious imagination and virtuosity, after a four-bar interpolation that sits squarely on the tonic (beginning at 2:51). Before Jackson's solo, the track consists of multiple iterations of the twelve-bar head, interspersed with three composed break-up strains that are a bit shorter (just eight bars each).[16]

The second item in the set, Lewis's "Blues in A Minor," unites some aspects of jazz and classical music by incorporating a procedure found in the works of Bach (and many other baroque composers). After a four-bar rhythmic pattern in triple meter, played on percussion instruments (bell, cymbal, and vibraphone), the bass enters with a twelve-bar melody that functions similarly to a basso ostinato (Example 4.4). This tune is repeated ten times, in common meter and embellished in various ways, serving as the foundation for a lengthy section of improvisation on the vibraphone and piano (0:40–4:45). Immediately thereafter, the piano, vibraphone, and bass play in unison a twelve-bar strain that effects an unexpected modulation to the submediant F major and sets the stage for a bass solo consisting of four choruses in the new key. A final set of surprises begins with the abrupt simultaneous return to A minor and triple meter at 6:37. Two unadorned iterations of the basso ostinato (identical to Example 4.4) follow a hair-raising sixteen-bar passage with a chromatic scale in the bass, which climbs a full octave upward from the dominant E.

The other two blues numbers were composed by Milt Jackson, and they feature his work on the vibraphone quite prominently. "Blues in H (B)" is the most conventional specimen on the album. After a four-bar introduction on the vibraphone, the twelve-bar head is heard twice, also on the vibraphone, but an octave higher the second time. There follows even more of Jackson's handiwork, four improvised choruses, which then are matched by Lewis's four choruses on the piano. The end of this cut is a mirror image of the beginning. Jackson plays the head twice, but in the upper octave first and then the lower. It is rounded off with a four-bar tag (tonally open-ended) that corresponds in length to the introduction.

The chief innovations of Jackson's "Blues in C Minor" are its thoroughgoing triple meter and its doubling of the twelve-bar blues format to twenty-four bars.[17] Otherwise, its overall structure hews very closely to that of his "Blues in H (B)." The core of "Blues in C Minor" consists of four choruses for vibraphone (1:27–4:02) and three for piano (4:02–5:59). The head is heard twice at the beginning—first as a regular waltz with straight quarter notes, then swung in the manner of a jazz waltz. The head also is played twice at the end, but the earlier eight-bar piano introduction is counterbalanced by two eight-bar tags, the second of which dissolves in a soulful rubato.

---

16. The first break-up strain (beginning at 0:48), which subsequently recurs as the outro at the end, features even more extensive chromatic motion than the head. The bass line moves downward by half steps from G to E-flat, with a striking pattern of octave leaps.

17. Knauer, *Zwischen Bebop und Free Jazz*, 1:102.

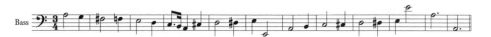

Example 4.4. "Blues in A Minor," bass ostinato (mm. 1–12).

Even though these four blues numbers partake of the time-honored tradition of using the pitches B-flat, A, C, and B-natural to pay homage to Bach by spelling out his name, they do so in a way that is certainly unusual and perhaps unique. There are hundreds of pieces that incorporate the chromatic pattern of Bach's name.[18] But it is possible that the Modern Jazz Quartet's tribute is the only one that involves four *movements* arranged in this sequence of tonalities rather than four individual notes.

Bach (and Not Bach) in *Blues on Bach*

The five odd-numbered tracks on Blues on Bach are versions of compositions by J. S. Bach—or, in one case, a piece that formerly had been attributed to Bach. They all were recorded one day before the blues numbers (on Monday, November 26, 1973), in the same location (Atlantic Recording Studios, New York). Track 3 on side 1 and the first track on side 2 are two of Bach's most widely recognized compositions.

The first is a setting of the chorale "Wachet auf, ruft uns die Stimme," which originated in 1731 as the middle movement (fourth of seven) of the church cantata BWV 140.[19] It subsequently was transcribed for organ and published in the late 1740s as one of the *Schübler Chorales*, BWV 645. The piece's title on Blues on Bach is "Rise Up in the Morning," which is similar to the original ("'Awake!' we are called by the voice").

The introduction is a rhythmic pattern played on the triangle against the background of handheld sleigh bells, which imitate the sound of birds in the early morning. The ritornello is assigned to the harpsichord, initially in just the right hand, and then with both hands in unison. The sixteenth notes are swung just slightly, the articulation in groups of three notes is distinctive and rather counterintuitive (see Example 4.5), and there are added beats between phrases (six extra beats of rest after the first two measures, and four extra beats after the next two). When the chorale cantus firmus enters, it is played on the harpsichord, and at that point the ritornello is transferred to the vibraphone.

18. A list that was compiled shortly before the last Bach Year, for instance, contains well over three hundred entries. See "BACH," in *Oxford Composer Companions: J. S. Bach*, ed. Malcolm Boyd (Oxford: Oxford University Press, 1999), 50–55.

19. Bach composed the cantata in Leipzig, for the Twenty-seventh Sunday after Trinity (25 November 1731). The work incorporates all three stanzas of Philipp Nicolai's chorale "Wachet auf, ruft uns die Stimme" (1599). The movement in question, "Zion hört die Wächter singen," originally was scored for tenor, strings (violins 1 and 2, viola) in unison, and basso continuo.

Example 4.5. "Rise Up in the Morning," beginning of ritornello
with John Lewis's articulation (mm. 1–2).

The remainder of the cut follows Bach's composition quite closely, with only a few minor exceptions. The MJQ omits the repeat of measures 1–21, presumably for reasons of expediency. Although this omission may well have been more suitable for modern sensibilities (similar, for instance, to omitting the repetition of expositions in twentieth-century performances of movements in sonata form), it also had the unfortunate and perhaps unintended consequence of altering the chorale's structure from AAB (bar form) to AB. A more benign and effective modification is heard at the end. In place of the penultimate measure, the MJQ plays a tag ending consisting of a threefold repetition of that measure. The third time, the latter half of the measure is played in augmentation (quarter notes instead of eighths), bringing the movement to a grand conclusion.

Two other departures from the Bachian exemplar concern details of performance practice. The bass does not enter until after the repetition of the first two-bar unit of the ritornello (m. 5 of Bach's original)—and when it does, the first six notes are played an octave higher than the pedal line in the *Schübler Chorales* version. Transposition to the upper octave is heard intermittently in the bass line throughout the movement, wherever the model approaches or exceeds the bass's lower limit of E_1. (Such rewriting to accommodate the range limits of instruments is a procedure that Bach himself also employed on a regular basis, in the process of adapting his own compositions.) Finally, the approach to ornamentation in the MJQ's rendition of "Wachet auf, ruft uns die Stimme" pulls in two different directions at the same time. On the one hand, there are a few extra notes here and there, as one might expect from jazz musicians. But there are also several spots that fairly beg for trills or other ornaments and are instead played in a plain and rather pedestrian manner.

Many of these observations apply as well to track 1 on side 2, titled "Precious Joy." This is an arrangement of the famous chorale setting that concludes both parts of the church cantata *Herz und Mund und Tat und Leben*, bwv 147, as movements 6 and 10 (two stanzas from Martin Janus's "Jesu, meiner Seelen Wonne"). Bach's composition was later popularized in a transcription for solo piano by Dame Myra Hess as "Jesu, Joy of Man's Desiring," and it is more likely this version than the original (scored for strings, voices, and continuo, with a pair of oboes doubling the first violin part and a trumpet doubling the soprano) that served as the model for Lewis's own reworking.[20]

20. J. S. Bach, *Jesu, Joy of Man's Desiring: Chorale from Cantata No. 147*, arranged for piano by Myra Hess (London: Oxford University Press, 1926).

The thread that runs throughout this piece, with only occasional interruptions, is the ritornello, played in steady triplets on the vibraphone. Milt Jackson's performance is astonishingly faithful to Bach's melody, introducing not even a single embellishment or alternate reading. Lewis's role, on the other hand, is mainly to play the chorale in quarter-note chords on the harpsichord, similar to Hess's version but with a few added rhythmic flourishes. He does, however, join forces with Jackson at the end to provide a jangly final iteration of the ritornello for vibraphone and harpsichord in unison.

The bass line is unobtrusive, moving predominantly in straight quarter notes and following Bach's original quite closely, albeit with minor deviations such as octave displacements similar to those noted in "Rise Up in the Morning." But the bass does perform a special function at the beginning. Instead of a rhythmic introduction, the arrangement begins with an unmeasured articulation of a low G, accompanied by the sound of sleigh bells. The bells continue through the entire cut, creating an effect similar to the Zimbelstern on some organs. The only other substantive departure from Bach's setting occurs at the end of the first and last ritornellos (at 0:21 and 3:03), where the final group of eighth-note triplets in each measure is augmented to quarter notes. This produces the odd (and, in my opinion, unsuccessful) transformation of the meter of these two measures from 3/4 to 5/4.

The models for the opening and closing numbers on *Blues on Bach* (track 1 on side 1 and track 5 on side 2) are not as well-known as those for "Rise Up in the Morning" and "Precious Joy," but they are hardly obscure. These arrangements have descriptive titles that superimpose new meanings on a pair of keyboard works by Bach. The album's opening selection is the chorale prelude "Das alte Jahr vergangen ist," BWV 614, from the *Orgelbüchlein*, which is renamed "Regret?" It is difficult to quantify the impact of the new title, but the addition of a question mark to a word with inherently negative connotations indicates that we are in unsettled territory. This appellation was undoubtedly inspired by the extreme chromaticism and ambiguous tonality of Bach's organ chorale, which produce a sense of longing and nostalgia.

Lewis's transcription for the MJQ is straightforward. The four contrapuntal lines—originally for the right hand of the organ (top), the left hand (middle two), and the pedal (bottom)—are reassigned to the right hand on the harpsichord, the vibraphone, the left hand on the harpsichord, and the bass (see Example 4.6). Comparison of measures 1–2 with the Bach original reveals that these jazz musicians made a few tiny changes of rhythm and ornamentation, but their rendition is otherwise a highly accurate facsimile. The role of percussion is understated but highly effective, consisting of only the striking of finger cymbals on most beats, beginning with the first downbeat, plus a brief flourish on the triangle to reinforce the last note (resolution of a 4–3 suspension).

The MJQ's interpretation of the Prelude in E-flat Minor from the first book of *The Well-Tempered Clavier*, BWV 853, which concludes the album, is even more evocative. The title "Tears from the Children" stimulates the imagination and provokes many

Example 4.6. "Regret?" (mm. 1–2).

(unanswerable) questions, such as, "Whose children?" and more importantly, "Why are they weeping?"

The musical means employed in this recording are familiar from the three cuts discussed above, although the harpsichord is more prominent than usual. The one-bar introduction consists of the three repeated half-note minor thirds of the left hand from measure 1 of the Bach prelude. When played in isolation on the harpsichord, these intervals sound brittle, especially since they are the first sonorities one hears. Thereafter, the harpsichord continues in its accompanimental role, sometimes altering the plodding half-note pulse to a livelier dotted quarter and eighth rhythm. Meanwhile, a lightly embellished form of the melody in measures 1–19, with its plentiful and soulful sixteenth notes, is spun out on the vibraphone. And the sleigh bells that contributed to the distinctive sound of "Rise Up in the Morning" are present (somewhat annoyingly) throughout this cut as well, entering simultaneously with the vibraphone.

The vibraphone takes a lengthy minute-long hiatus in measures 20–28 (2:06–3:05), which shines the spotlight on the harpsichord in a rather unflattering fashion. To my ear, this passage—with just harpsichord, bass, and the incessant sleigh bells—is unpleasantly shrill, especially in the context of a jazz recording. The vibraphone drops out again near the end (after 3:51) but rejoins for the final cadence and contributes a shimmering arpeggio to the last chord, a Picardy third.

Finally, track 3 on side 2 is a three-voice fugue in D minor, which is supplied with the title "Don't Stop This Train," largely on account of the driving rhythm that is set in motion from the very beginning on suspended cymbals. The introduction is a one-bar passage in which the pattern of a sixteenth note followed by two thirty-seconds is beaten out repeatedly. The drummer Connie Kay continues using this specific cymbal until the beginning of the fugal answer at the midpoint of measure 4, where he switches to a different suspended cymbal. Kay's cymbal work on the cut, which reinforces the successive entries of subject and answer in the fugue, is summarized in Table 4.1.

Table 4.1. "Don't Stop This Train" structure and instrumentation

Introduction and mm. 1–4a	cymbal 1	subject – harpsichord
mm. 4b–7	cymbal 2	answer – vibraphone
mm. 8–11a	cymbal 1[a]	subject – bass
mm. 11b–14	cymbal 2	answer – harpsichord
mm. 15–18	cymbal 1	subject – vibraphone
mm. 19–21	cymbal 2	episode
mm. 22–28	alternation between cymbals 1 and 2	subject – bass; coda

[a] The instrument in this passage and in mm. 15–18 is nearly inaudible and may possibly be a third cymbal.

The fugue's three voices are assigned to the harpsichord, vibraphone, and bass. The initial statement of the subject is on the harpsichord, and Lewis plays it with an eccentric articulation similar to what was observed earlier in the ritornello of "Rise Up in the Morning" (see Example 4.7). The middle voice is played on the harpsichord more or less as written, with only a few added or altered notes. The registration of the instrument does expand, however, from a single 8' set of strings in measures 1–8, to two sets in measures 9–21, and a third set (or possibly octave doubling in the left hand) for measures 22–28. The vibraphone faithfully executes the upper voice, albeit with a few more extra notes and alterations than in the harpsichord line. The bottom voice is played by the bass—nearly without any adjustments, for once, since almost every note of its line lies within the instrument's normal range. The single exception is the final note, D_1, which is a whole step below the bass's lowest string (E_1). This anomaly explains the note's initially sour intonation. Bassist Percy Heath apparently used his tuning peg to lower the pitch after first plucking the higher (wrong) note. One assumes that this was done on purpose—and it may well have been interesting to view in person—but it unfortunately mars the ending and therefore seems ill-advised.

It is ironic that this fugue, one of just five pieces that the MJQ chose for its tribute to J. S. Bach, turns out not to have been composed by him. The claim on the album cover notwithstanding ("based on Bach's Fugue in D Minor from the 'Clavierbuechlein'"), this work is BWV Anh. 180, which is attributed to Bach in some manuscript sources but actually was written by Johann Peter Kellner (1705–72).[21] There is nothing inherently

21. See Wolfgang Schmieder, *Thematisch-systematisches Verzeichnis der musikalischen Werke von Johann Sebastian Bach: Bach-Werke-Verzeichnis (BWV)*, rev. ed. (Wiesbaden: Breitkopf & Härtel, 1990), 181; and NBA V/12, *Werke zweifelhafter Echtheit für Tasteninstrumente*, KB, ed. Ulrich Bartels and Frieder Rempp (Kassel: Bärenreiter, 2006), 282–84. Also Georg Feder, "Bemerkungen über einige J. S. Bach zugeschriebene Werke," *Die Musikforschung* 11 (1958): 77–78. In addition to the sources listed in these publications, BWV Anh. 180 is found in a manuscript collection of *Suiten und Fugen von J. S. Bach* that was acquired by Yale University in 2010 (Yale University, Beinecke Library, Music Deposit 88). A digital copy is available at https://brbl-dl.library.yale.edu/vufind/Record/3882373 (accessed 12 July 2018).

Example 4.7. "Don't Stop This Train," fugal subject with
John Lewis's articulation (mm. 1–4).

implausible about the style of this composition that ought to have raised questions about its authenticity. It is a perfectly serviceable fugue, and its composer was, after all, well acquainted with Bach and his music.[22] But given the fact that there are literally hundreds of fugues by Bach from which to choose, it seems doubly ironic that this was not the first time the MJQ had selected a spurious piece. A decade earlier the group recorded with the guitarist Laurindo Almeida the Fugue in A Minor, BWV 947, which David Schulenberg has argued "is almost certainly not [Bach's] work."[23]

Blues on Bach: Instrumentation, Adaptation, Cover Art

This section considers general aspects of *Blues on Bach* that are germane to the project as a whole. An arresting aspect of the sound of the Bach arrangements is John Lewis's use of the harpsichord. Especially because of its alternation with the piano, from one track to the next, the harpsichord serves as a potent marker of the imagined baroque. The piano in the four blues numbers anchors this album in the jazz idiom, while the harpsichord points toward some sort of Other—not exactly exotic, but certainly unusual in this context.[24]

The notion of most jazz keyboardists blithely toggling between piano and harpsichord seems downright bizarre (try to imagine Art Tatum or Thelonious Monk doing so). Yet it probably seemed unremarkable to Lewis, who in 1962 had married the Yugoslavian harpsichordist Mirjana Vrbanić, and with whom he later recorded a version of the Goldberg Variations.[25] Not surprisingly, then, the harpsichord was a common household item for Lewis. Gary Giddins, who was personally acquainted with all four

22. See Russell Stinson, *The Bach Manuscripts of Johann Peter Kellner and His Circle: A Case Study in Reception History* (Durham: Duke University Press, 1989).

23. David Schulenberg, *The Keyboard Music of J. S. Bach*, 2nd ed. (New York: Routledge, 2006), 440. The Modern Jazz Quartet with Laurindo Almeida, *Collaboration*, Atlantic 1429, 1964, 33⅓ rpm.

24. The MJQ's embrace of the harpsichord may also have been spurred by the "baroque rock" phenomenon of the 1960s. I am indebted to Daniel R. Melamed for this suggestion. See Sara Gulgas, "Looking Forward to the Past: Baroque Rock's Postmodern Nostalgia and the Politics of Memory" (Ph.D. diss., University of Pittsburgh, 2017).

25. John Lewis and Mirjana Lewis, *The Chess Game: Based on J. S. Bach's "The Goldberg Variations,"* part 1, Philips 832 015–1, 1987, 33⅓ rpm; part 2, Philips 832 588–1, 1987, 33⅓ rpm.

members of the MJQ, provided the following vivid description of Lewis's apartment in New York: "Walking into his home was like walking into a very well-kept-up museum. He had a Japanese screen, some terrific paintings, including a 1955 Miró that he was very proud of. The apartment was filled with sculpted birds, a quill pen, brass bell, antique reading glasses, bowls and goblets from all over the world. And he had two grand pianos, a Steinway and a Bechstein, and a fantastic-looking harpsichord."[26]

A second facet of *Blues on Bach* that deserves additional scrutiny is the language used on the cover to describe the Bach arrangements. As mentioned earlier, each cut was given a new title, and they were said to have been "based on" various works by Bach. But it is worth considering what this actually means. To say that one work is "based on" another normally leads one to expect more liberties than are taken here. Indeed, it would be more accurate to characterize them as faithful transcriptions of Bach's compositions, with only a few very minor changes here and there.

Every part of all five models is present in the MJQ versions, and they are performed in the original keys. This is true even of "Tears from the Children," a transcription of a prelude in E-flat minor (six flats), which is a decidedly uncommon key for jazz musicians. It seems likely that the new titles and the claim that these versions were "based on," rather than transcriptions of, Bach's music were designed for a business purpose—namely, to ensure that composer royalties accrued to Lewis for these tracks.[27]

Third, the album's cover art merits brief examination. It almost goes without saying, but probably ought to be mentioned at the outset, that the predominant color on both the front and back sides of the cover is blue. In view of the album's title, a competent graphic designer would likely have had little choice in this matter. In addition to the name of the combo and the title of the album, the front is dominated by portraits of the individual participants (see Figure 4.1). On the left and right are head shots of the members of the MJQ, two on each side, in tall and narrow panels. The fifth and central panel is wider than the others, has a reddish hue (in contrast to the surrounding blue), and most importantly is intended to depict the face of J. S. Bach. Once again, though, the MJQ inadvertently stepped into a pitfall, for the image that was selected is "the portrait of an unidentified middle-aged man painted by Johann Jacob Ihle," which is on display at the Bach House museum in Eisenach. Christoph Wolff dismissed the flimsy attempts to link this painting to J. S. Bach since the late nineteenth century with

26. Gary Giddins, "Origins of the MJQ: John Lewis's Precepts about Improvisation, Tempo, Structure, and Presentation" (lecture, presented at MJQ Redux: A Modern Jazz Quartet Symposium at Sewanee, University of the South, Sewanee, Tenn., 10 February 2018). I am grateful to Stephen R. Miller for making available a recording of this symposium.

27. I owe this insight to Dwight D. Andrews.

Figure 4.1. Front cover of *Blues on Bach*. Reproduced with permission.

the following blunt assessment: "Pure fantasy—not interpretive scholarship however carefully reasoned—created a completely fictional fact."[28]

Fortunately, the back of the album cover is on firmer ground (see Figure 4.2). Again, four photographs of the musicians—this time with their instruments—flank a facsimile of the autograph of the first movement of Bach's Sonata in G Minor for Unaccompanied Violin, BWV 1001.[29] The track listings are given at the top of the middle panel, above Bach's handwriting, and the letters of the key signatures for the blues numbers (B, A, C, H) are printed in white, so they can be plainly seen.

---

28. Christoph Wolff, "Images of Bach in the Perspective of Basic Research and Interpretative Scholarship," *Journal of Musicology* 22 (2005): 507. A succinct account of the painting's history can be found in Werner Neumann, *Bilddokumente zur Lebensgeschichte Johann Sebastian Bachs*, Bach-Dokumente 4 (Kassel: Bärenreiter, 1979), 359–60.

29. Berlin, Staatsbibliothek zu Berlin—Preußischer Kulturbesitz, Musikabteilung mit Mendelssohn-Archiv, Mus. ms. Bach P 967. The facsimile of this page (fol. 2r) was evidently rolled up, or distorted in some other manner, so that all eleven staves would fit in the available space.

Figure 4.2. Back cover of *Blues on Bach*. Reproduced with permission.

Three Milestones

Within one year after the recording sessions for *Blues on Bach* (November 26–27, 1973), the MJQ achieved three career milestones. The first came a month later, on December 28, when the combo performed with the Juilliard String Quartet at Carnegie Hall. It was hardly unprecedented for a jazz group to appear in Carnegie Hall. Benny Goodman had done so thirty-five years earlier.[30] And the MJQ itself had recorded a live album there in 1966.[31] It was a bit more unusual, however, for two preeminent ensembles in the classical and jazz worlds to share the stage. According to an announcement in the *New York Times*, the idea for the concert originated a few months earlier, when both groups were on tour in South America and John Lewis met Robert Mann, the string quartet's first violinist. The Juilliard's contribution to the Carnegie Hall event was Schubert's String Quartet No. 14 in D Minor ("Death and the Maiden"). The MJQ,

30. See Catherine Tackley, *Benny Goodman's Famous 1938 Carnegie Hall Jazz Concert* (New York: Oxford University Press, 2012).

31. The Modern Jazz Quartet, *Blues at Carnegie Hall*, Atlantic 1468, 1966, 33⅓ rpm.

on the other hand, performed the repertoire it had just recorded (minus Lewis's "Blues in B Flat" and "Blues in A Minor"), which the newspaper described as "'Bach and the Blues,' consisting of seven pieces: Mr. Lewis's adaptation to jazz rhythms of several Bach chorales and preludes and two blues pieces by Milt Jackson." The two quartets also united for a joint performance of unidentified works by Lewis and Gunther Schuller.[32]

About six months later, *Blues on Bach* received the kind of critical acclaim that most musicians can only dream of. It was awarded the maximum five-star rating in the premier jazz magazine, *Down Beat*. Furthermore, the review began by describing the album as "a classic, the recording of all that the MJQ is about: the timeless beauty of music," and it concluded with the declaration that this project was the group's "masterpiece."[33]

The third milestone had an air of finality about it, because it was the MJQ's last concert before the quartet disbanded after twenty-two years together. The performance took place in Avery Fisher Hall in New York on November 25, 1974—one year, nearly to the day, after the *Blues on Bach* recording sessions—and LPs and compact discs were subsequently issued on the Atlantic label.[34] As is to be expected, the set list included numbers that the MJQ had played since the beginning (such as "Softly, as in a Morning Sunrise"). But the group also performed three selections from *Blues on Bach*: Lewis's "Blues in A Minor" and "Tears from the Children" and Jackson's "Blues in H (B)." Given the MJQ's fidelity to the text of Bach's Prelude in E-flat Minor, the live version of "Tears from the Children" is similar to the recording in most respects. But the sound of the concert performance lacks the harshness noted earlier, and is therefore more pleasant, because a modern piano was used instead of a harpsichord.

John Lewis's *Well-Tempered Clavier*

About a decade later, Lewis was approached by the Japanese record company Nippon Phonogram about recording Bach's *Well-Tempered Clavier*, a project he began in January 1984 and which ultimately was issued in four volumes on the Philips label from 1985 (Bach's 300th birthday) to 1990.[35] His coproducer was the critic, journalist, and radio

---

32. "Going Out Guide," *New York Times*, 28 December 1973.

33. Michael Bourne, review of *Blues on Bach*, *Down Beat* 41.12 (20 June 1974): 18.

34. The Modern Jazz Quartet, *The Last Concert*, Atlantic 2–909, 1975, 33⅓ rpm, double album (fourteen selections); *More from the Last Concert*, Atlantic 8806, 1981, 33⅓ rpm (six selections); *The Complete Last Concert*, Atlantic 81976-2, 1989, two compact discs (twenty-two selections, including two bonus tracks).

35. John Lewis, *J. S. Bach, Preludes and Fugues from The Well-Tempered Clavier, Book 1*, vol. 1, Philips 824 381–1, 1985, 33⅓ rpm (nos. 1, 2, 6, 7, 21, 22); vol. 2, Philips 826 698–1, 1986, 33⅓ rpm (nos. 9, 4, 5, 16, 8); vol. 3, Philips 836 821–2, 1989, compact disc (nos. 3, 10, 11, 13, 15, 19); vol. 4, Philips PHCE-3030, 1990, compact disc (nos. 12, 14, 17, 18, 20, 23, 24). The fine print on the back covers of

host Kiyoshi Koyama, a leading figure in Japan's postwar jazz scene.[36] This was Lewis's opportunity to unite his music with Bach's in a more organic manner than on the *Blues on Bach* album. He attempted the task with some trepidation, noting that it "has demanded a great deal of preparation on my part, both in the form of piano practice and in the form of compositional work."[37] Lewis's extensive planning even involved a vigorous effort to locate and make use of the very best critical edition. To this end, he scheduled a luncheon meeting with Christoph Wolff at the Harvard Faculty Club to discuss the intricacies of the Neue Bach-Ausgabe.[38]

These recordings deserve greater scrutiny than is possible here. But a brief description of the Prelude and Fugue No. 1 in C Major, BWV 846, will serve to illustrate what is afoot. For the preludes, Lewis's standard procedure was to play Bach's music straightforwardly until near the end of the movement, then to take a brief detour into jazz improvisation, before returning to Bach's score at the end. The order of events for his rendition of the Prelude in C Major is as follows. First, Lewis plays nearly the entire piece as Bach wrote it, departing from the score only in the second half of measure 31 (1:20). Thereupon, instead of proceeding to the final four bars, he returns to the beginning and improvises for about forty-five seconds (1:20–2:05), using Bach's chord progression in measures 1–17 as his harmonic framework. He then returns to Bach's score in measure 18 (2:05), this time following it all the way to the end.

The Fugue in C Major follows a similar pattern, but each of the four contrapuntal lines is assigned to a different instrument: violin, piano, guitar, and bass.[39] Lewis nearly

---

these releases identifies this project as "'The Bridge Game' based on J. S. Bach's 'The Well-Tempered Clavier' Book 1, composed by John Lewis," and some of them include subtitles alluding to playing cards, such as "One Spade" on vol. 2 (an alternative version of the Prelude No. 5, also known as "Tears from the Children").

36. Katherine Whatley, "Kiyoshi Koyama: A Life Lived with Jazz," *Japan Times*, 29 March 2018.

37. John Lewis, "J. S. Bach's Influence on My Work," liner notes for compact disc release of *J. S. Bach, Preludes and Fugues from The Well-Tempered Clavier, Book 1*, vol. 1, Philips 824 381–2, 1985.

38. Christoph Wolff, e-mail message to author, 13 July 2018. The intermediary who established contact between Lewis and Wolff was H. Roderick Nordell (Harvard College '46), a good friend of Wolff's who knew Lewis very well and for a long time.

39. The violinist for vols. 1 and 2 was Joel Lester, distinguished music theorist, longtime dean of the Mannes College of Music, and author of *Bach's Works for Solo Violin: Style, Structure, Performance* (New York: Oxford University Press, 1999). At the inception of this project, Lester and Lewis were faculty colleagues at the City College of New York, and Lewis invited Lester's participation. Lester, in turn, recruited the violist Lois Martin, when a fifth part was required. The other two regular participants in the fugues were Howard Collins (guitar) and Marc Johnson (bass). I am grateful to Joel Lester for an informative phone interview on 26 November 2017.

Table 4.2. Analytical comparison of John Lewis's arrangement of
Bach's Fugue in C Major with original

LEWIS	BACH		
mm. 1–23	mm. 1–23	0:00–1:39	
mm. 24–30a	mm. 1–7a	1:39–2:07	Subject played on piano instead of violin
mm. 30b–33	[improvisation]	2:07–2:22	
mm. 34–37	mm. 7–10	2:22–2:39	
mm. 38–41a	[improvisation]	2:39–2:55	
mm. 41b–45a	mm. 10b–14a	2:55–3:12	
mm. 45b–93a	[improvisation]	3:12–6:42	Twelve four-bar choruses
mm. 93b–106	mm. 14b–27	6:42–7:50	

quadruples the length of the fugue (from 27 bars to 106) by repeating material and adding three improvisatory passages (see Table 4.2). The centerpiece of this procedure is a set of twelve choruses, which occupies almost half of the track's total recording time, and which unfortunately does not rank among Lewis's more inspired moments. It is preceded by two brief passages that also are improvised but that are embedded into Lewis's performance of Bach's text.[40] In essence, the entire fugue is played twice. The first iteration stops four bars short of the end, and the second includes the improvisatory material and some overlapping and dovetailing of Bach's and Lewis's contributions.[41]

Outlook

John Lewis's and the Modern Jazz Quartet's engagement with the legacy of J. S. Bach provides an ideal arena for grappling with a variety of complex issues. In addition to the musical matters in the foreground of this study, it is important to consider more fully what exactly is at stake when four African American jazz musicians devote such

40. A fairly reliable transcription of Lewis's improvisations in this fugue can be found in Udo Zilkens, *Johann Sebastian Bach: Zwischen Zahlenmystik und Jazz: Die Eröffnung des Wohltemperierten Klaviers im Spiegel ihrer Interpretationen durch Musiktheoretiker und Musiker, in Kunstwerken und Bearbeitungen* (Cologne-Rodenkirchen: Tonger, 1996), 53.

41. Since his *Well-Tempered Clavier* was clearly a labor of love and the culmination of several decades of engagement with Bach's music, Lewis must have been sorely disappointed with the *New York Times'* review of the first volume, which read in part, "It's puzzling . . . to hear an album gone so wrong. . . . On his Bach album, Mr. Lewis's genuine affection for the composer doesn't come through his playing. With the ensemble, and sometimes by himself, he makes Bach sound like background music." Jon Pareles, "John Lewis's Piano and Bach's Clavier," *New York Times*, 11 August 1985.

a significant amount of their creative effort to a German composer more than two centuries and a world apart from twentieth-century America. Samuel Floyd got the ball rolling some years ago when he made the following trenchant observation about the MJQ and similar groups: "For those who were emotionally and ideologically committed to the African-American side of the musical mix, many of the products of the cool/Third Stream trend were viewed either as vapid cultural irrelevancies or as musical, social, and cultural threats to 'real' black music."[42] Scholars such as Christopher Coady and Kelsey Klotz have recently picked up the gauntlet and made significant contributions to this inquiry.[43] But a judicious and nuanced view of this thorny problem will require additional perspectives and still lies some distance in the future.

42. Samuel A. Floyd Jr., *The Power of Black Music: Interpreting Its History from Africa to the United States* (New York: Oxford University Press, 1995), 167.

43. Christopher Coady, *John Lewis and the Challenge of "Real" Black Music* (Ann Arbor: University of Michigan Press, 2016); Kelsey A. K. Klotz, "Racial Ideologies in 1950s Cool Jazz" (Ph.D. diss., Washington University in St. Louis, 2016).

Certifying J. S. Bach's Interplanetary Funksmanship; or, What Bach Meant to Bernie Worrell

Ellen Exner

FOR JUDIE

In his 2014 memoir, *Brothas Be, Yo Like George, Ain't That Funkin' Kinda Hard on You?*, George Clinton, infamous leader of a constellation of bands referred to collectively as Parliament-Funkadelic—or more commonly, P-Funk—specifically identified the contrapuntal style of J. S. Bach as a particular stimulus behind the composition of the track "Nappy Dugout" from Funkadelic's 1973 album, *Cosmic Slop*:

> There's "Nappy Dugout," a vicious, low-groove that Boogie brought us wedded to a lyrical idea I got from something a girl said to me about pussy.[1] Boogie's track was so funky that I didn't have to add too many words to it; my job was to make my point and get out of the way. The final step was to let Bernie take his shot at it, add his keyboard parts around the bass. Bernie, like Sly, liked Bach quite a bit, and both of them used his theory of counterpoint, which is about setting melodies up on top of one another to create something larger. Bernie's understanding was a bit more classical than Sly's, but both had a way of making different parts that wove in and out of each other.[2]

The Boogie whom Clinton refers to is Cordell "Boogie" Mosson, P-Funk's bassist. Sly is Sylvester Stone of the band Sly and the Family Stone, and Bernie is Dr. George Bernard Worrell Jr. (1944–2016), the brilliant keyboardist and music director of Parliament-Funkadelic.

---

1. Funkadelic, *Cosmic Slop*, Westbound WB 2022, 1973, 33⅓ rpm. To clarify, "Nappy Dugout" is slang for female genitalia.

2. George Clinton, *Brothas Be, Yo Like George, Ain't That Funkin' Kinda Hard on You?* (New York: Atria, 2014), 118.

According to Rickey Vincent, prize-winning author of *Funk: The Music, the People, and the Rhythm of the One*, "P-Funk remains the strongest influence on black music since their popular zenith in 1978."[3] The group is so significant a force that Prince himself inducted it into the Rock & Roll Hall of Fame in 1997. P-Funk's dominance is plainly evident in how often its tracks are sampled by other musicians: Dr. Dre, Snoop Dogg, De la Soul, and many other rap, R&B, and hip-hop artists have used P-Funk's music as the basis for their own new compositions. Legal issues aside, sampling is an act of homage to revered artists, and P-Funk ranks among the most sampled bands of all time.[4]

If Bach is somehow in P-Funk's musical DNA, as Clinton claims, and P-Funk's sound has been foundational for a new generation of popular music artists, then Bach's musical influence informs canonic masterworks not just of the concert hall but also of funk, hip-hop, and rap. Thus, Clinton's specific reference to Bach's influence on Worrell, P-Funk's main musical engine, cannot pass unexamined.[5] This group, once described "as a psychedelic rock band with diapers, dashikis and face paint,"[6] is hardly the obvious place to look for the influence of the Leipzig Thomaskantor. Engaged listening across the band's discography makes it clear, though, that there is ample musically intelligent life on board the iconic P-Funk Mothership, and it emanates most powerfully from

---

3. Rickey Vincent, *Funk: The Music, the People, and the Rhythm of the One*, with a foreword by George Clinton (New York: St. Martin's Griffin, 1996), 231.

4. A list of P-Funk tracks sampled by other musicians can be found on the website "Who Sampled: Exploring the DNA of Music," accessed 5 June 2019, https://www.whosampled.com/song-tag/P-Funk/. The list includes 128 borrowings. "Nappy Dugout" itself has been sampled by such artists as Ice Cube, A Tribe Called Quest, and Dru Down: https://www.whosampled.com/search/?q=Nappy+dugout. According to Justin Avery of the *Houston Press*, "George Clinton ranks second on the list of most-sampled artists in music history" ("Top 5 Most Sampled George Clinton Songs," 20 February 2013, accessed 5 June 2019, https://www.houstonpress.com/music/top-5-most-sampled-george-clinton -songs-6780084).

5. Investigation of Clinton's reference to Bach's influence on Sly Stone will have to wait, though, for another occasion. For now, the curious might be interested in viewing part 8 of *Small Talk about Sly*, a series of interviews about the musical background and contributions of one of funk's greatest innovators, Sylvester Stone. Part 8 of the series focuses on the concept of counterpoint as taught by David Froehlich, the junior college harmony instructor whom Stone called the "most inspirational teacher of my life." That quotation can be found in Mike Corpos's article "Students, Friends Gather to Remember SCC Music Teacher Froehlich," *Daily Republic*, 9 June 2013, accessed 20 September 2019, https://www.dailyrepublic.com/all-dr-news/solano-news/education-news/students-friends -gather-to-remember-scc-music-teacher-froehlich/. Part 8 of the film ("Counterpoint and Bach" by Greg Zola) can be viewed on YouTube: https://youtu.be/bZZ2-XnbIp8.

6. Marc Weingarten, "George Clinton's Funk Chronicle, 'Brothas Be, Yo Like George,'" review of Clinton, *Brothas Be*, *Los Angeles Times*, 31 October 2014.

Worrell's keyboard section.[7] Research into his extensive musical background reveals that there is most definitely Bach in your funk, and a lot more besides. This essay is an exploration of P-Funk's incalculable (and unpaid)[8] musical debt to Worrell, by way of what Clinton called "Bach." As such, it joins an ever-expanding discussion of how Bach's music transcends generic and cultural boundaries. Indeed, similar things could be (and have been) said of P-Funk.[9]

Bernie Worrell's path to P-Funk was in no way predictable. The "Wizard of Woo," as he became known, was a classically trained keyboard virtuoso and former child prodigy.[10] He was born in Long Branch, New Jersey, and raised in nearby Plainfield, where (to his mother's great dismay) he first met George Clinton, who ran the local barbershop.[11] Worrell's extraordinary musical talent was evident and storied early on:

7. The reference here is to P-Funk's "Mothership"/extraterrestrial narrative, created by Clinton and bassist Bootsy Collins (also famous for his collaborations with James Brown) following what they reportedly thought was a UFO sighting on their way home from a gig (Vincent, *Funk*, 240). The result was the band's fourth album, *The Mothership Connection* (Casablanca NBLP 7022, 1975, 33⅓ rpm), which has since gone platinum. In full embrace of the spectacle generated by the extraterrestrial storyline, P-Funk's concerts thereafter began with an outrageously illuminated model spaceship (The Mothership) that delivered George Clinton to the stage in the form of the alien "Dr. Funkenstein." The idea was that Funkenstein descended in order to spread funk's universal love message of The One—the thing that unites us all, which also happens to be the rhythmic goal in this musical idiom. The religious overtones are clear. The Mothership itself is now in the Smithsonian Museum of African American History and Culture.

The present essay's title engages with a central concept from the band's adopted universal/cosmic narrative—"the more you feel The Funk, the closer you get to a transcendent level" (Vincent, *Funk*, 242)—and the song lyric "the desired effect is what you get when you improve your interplanetary funksmanship" (from "P-Funk [Wants to Get Funked Up]" on *The Mothership Connection*).

8. According to Judie Worrell, George Clinton cheated her late husband Bernie out of the considerable royalties to which he should have been entitled for his indispensable work with the band. The lawsuit is in progress. The details of their story can be found here: http://wooniversaltruths.bernieworrell .com/, accessed 20 September 2019. I would like to thank Mrs. Worrell for all of her kind support of this essay despite its necessary inclusion of Clinton's commentary on her husband's art.

9. See, for example, Vincent, *Funk*, esp. 235, 240.

10. His biography, discography, and other information can be found on his official website: bernie worrell.com.

11. Clinton describes the scene and the community of musicians that gathered around him in Plain-field on pp. 21–31 of *Brothas Be*. He offers more detail about his initial contact with Worrell on pp. 58–60, including how upset Bernie's mother was over their budding relationship. Clinton gets a few details wrong in the retelling. For example, he claims that Bernie studied at the Berklee College of Music in Boston when, in reality, it was the New England Conservatory. He also misspells the name of Worrell's wife, which is not Judy, but Judie.

in Clinton's words, "he was a local Mozart who wrote his first symphony before he was in junior high. . . . He could do anything from Ray Charles to classical music."[12] Worrell's mother, Cora, a domestic worker and church musician, fostered it in every way that she could, finding her gifted son excellent private teachers and sending him to piano lessons at the Juilliard School in New York before he left for college.

According to Worrell's successful application to the New England Conservatory of Music in 1962, it had been his dream "to do piano, orchestra, and concert work," with the hope of gaining "a graduate degree to teach music on a college level."[13] The universe had other plans for him, though, and that youthful goal remained unrealized. He was seven and a half semesters into his classical piano performance degree when he was forced suddenly to drop out of school due to the unexpected death of his father. Almost immediately, Worrell became musical director for the soul singer Maxine Brown for a little over two years before answering Clinton's call from the Apollo Theater inviting him to join P-Funk. His first album with the group was its second: *Free Your Mind and Your Ass Will Follow* (1970).[14] After leaving Clinton's bands, Worrell worked with such artists as Keith Richards, the Talking Heads, the Pretenders, and actress Meryl Streep, who said of him, "Kindness comes off that man like stardust."[15] The former concert pianist was inducted into the Rock & Roll Hall of Fame twice and is listed there, along with Parliament-Funkadelic, as one of contemporary rap and

12. Ibid., 58–59. According to Worrell himself, it wasn't a symphony that he wrote in junior high but a piano concerto at the age of eight. See Matt Rogers, "Bernie Worrell Was the Key to the P-Funk Sound," in *Wax Poetics*, accessed 9 April 2019, http://www.waxpoetics.com/blog/features/articles/bernie-worrell-key-p-funk-sound/?fbclid=IwAR0x5XvLDo6fePTPt7peZeJT41KhQO-C1YHB_Q9f9YSogLODzavYcjhQxuk. The article was originally published as "The Synthesizer," *Wax Poetics*, August/September 2006.

13. George Bernard Worrell Jr., Admissions Application: Personal Statement, dated 8 June 1962, New England Conservatory of Music (registrar's office). Accessed with the kind permission of Judie Worrell. I thank also Alexander Wolniak and Robert Winkley of the New England Conservatory registrar's office for their excellent cooperation.

14. Westbound Records, WB 2001, 33⅓ rpm. This album's credo was quoted by Susan McClary in her description of the function of dance at Louis XIV's court, with the point that Louis's philosophy was actually quite the opposite of George Clinton's. Louis preferred to control the mind by way of controlling the body through protocols such as strictly ordered dance. McClary, "Unruly Passions and Court Dances: Technology of the Body in Baroque Music," in *From the Royal to the Republican Body*, ed. Sara E. Melzer and Kathryn Norberg (Berkeley: UC Berkeley Press, 1998), 85–112 (esp. 88).

15. Associated Press, "Bernie Worrell, Parliament-Funkadelic Co-founder, Dies Aged 72," *The Guardian*, 24 June 2016, accessed 18 March 2019, https://www.theguardian.com/music/2016/jun/25/bernie-worrell-parliament-funkadelic-co-founder-dies-aged-72. Streep and Worrell worked together on her 2015 movie *Ricki and the Flash*.

R&B's "most sampled musicians ever."[16] In May 2019, he, along with P-Funk, received a lifetime achievement Grammy Award (posthumously).

Worrell's virtuosic instrumental commentary, encyclopedic command of musical styles, contagious bass lines, and the extraterrestrial soundscape he pioneered with his Moog synthesizers not only created P-Funk's signature sound but functioned as the glue holding the multifarious ensemble together. The infusion of classical idioms into P-Funk's eclectic blend, although seldom described, was among Worrell's essential contributions. His accumulated musical experience and enormous professional success eventually made him the recipient of that once-desired professor's degree, an honorary doctorate, from his alma mater, the New England Conservatory (NEC). Sadly, the gesture came just weeks before his death due to cancer in June 2016.

Rigorous formal training and innate musical curiosity meant that Worrell was intimately familiar with the canonical works of the Western art tradition and the principles of formal composition. He brought his deep knowledge and extraordinary skills to Parliament-Funkadelic, a group of bands whose style range is so eclectic that it spawned its own adjective: P-Funk. P-Funk is often described as a mixture of pop, rock, Motown, rhythm and blues, funk, and soul, but a focus on Worrell's contributions demonstrates that J. S. Bach and other traditionally European concert hall idioms belong in that list as well.[17] The singular union of these many styles into one is what creates the P-Funk and makes it like no other. Worrell rendered the audacious multiplicity coherent.

Clinton's initially arresting claim that the music of "Nappy Dugout" was somehow inspired by Bachian compositional techniques suddenly becomes utterly plausible in light of Worrell's background. The musical style of "Nappy Dugout" nevertheless remains an obstacle to corroborating Clinton's recollection. The song does indeed feature the "vicious low groove" and sparse vocals he described in his autobiography, but the compositional logic is only contrapuntal in the most generous of senses. In fact, the song is explicit in every way except Bachian.[18] The musical texture of the song is not generated by counterpoint. Instead, it is an example of polyphony: the track is composed of multiple, independent, layered musical lines. Thus, it certainly does contain "melodies up on top of one another," as Clinton claimed, but there is no calculated, note-against-note counterpoint in the manner descriptive of Bach's art.

16. "Bernard Worrell," GeorgeClinton.com, accessed 1 October 2016, http://georgeclinton.com/family/bernie-worrell/.

17. Vincent (*Funk*, 235) briefly discusses the cultural implications of P-Funk's mixture of traditionally European and African American idioms (many by way of Worrell). He concludes that P-Funk "transcended" W. E. B. Du Bois's concept of "two warring ideals [the African American and the European] in one black body" to produce "the *ultimate* in African-American liberation" (emphasis original).

18. The full text can be found here: Genius.com, https://genius.com/Funkadelic-nappy-dugout-lyrics (accessed 20 September 2019).

If the technical details do not bear out Clinton's assertion that Bachian counterpoint informed "Nappy Dugout," we can still be reasonably sure that Worrell, a conservatory-trained concert pianist, encountered Bach's music.[19] We can therefore impugn the details of Clinton's recollection in this case while continuing the search for the claim's basis: there is some truth behind it even if the facts got muddled in the retelling. There are, in fact, multiple songs within P-Funk's discography that betray significant "classical" influences—even specifically baroque ones. For example, "O Lord, Why Lord/Prayer," an early track by a subsection of P-Funk known as Parliament,[20] features Worrell on harpsichord. He improvises over Pachelbel's famous Canon in D to accompany lyrics that are a passionate meditation on the scourge of racism.[21] Canon is a particularly poignant compositional choice for underpinning these lyrics because its chief characteristic is perpetual, relentless return despite appearances of forward progress. In addition, few pieces of music could be more suggestive of cultural privilege and European tradition than Pachelbel's Canon, so the conflict of topics contained in this song—the desperate frustration of a senselessly oppressed people paired with a musical style traditionally associated with the oppressors—is profoundly, devastatingly moving. Because the track is a cover, Worrell was not responsible for the original concept, but he was responsible for Parliament's arrangement of it[22] as well as

---

19. Exposure to Bach's music would not have been limited to performance repertory. Conservatory students also take courses in harmony, counterpoint, and composition. Worrell received advanced training in these subjects even before entering NEC. According to an interview he gave in 2006, he had four years of instruction from John F. Noge at the New York College of Music. See Rogers, "Bernie Worrell Was the Key."

20. Originally released on the album *Osmium*, Invictus Records ST-7302, 1970, 33⅓ rpm.

21. The first two stanzas:

> I've searched the open sky
> To find the reason why
> Oh Lord, why Lord
>
> The color of my skin
> Is said to be an awful sin
> Oh Lord, why Lord.

The rest can be found on Genius.com, https://genius.com/Parliament-oh-lord-why-lord-prayer-lyrics (accessed 10 June 2019). Parliament's version is a cover of an original by the Spanish group (Los) Pop Tops. The lyrics are by Jean Marcel Bouchety and Phil Trim. Intriguingly, the B side of the original release single is "The Voice of the Dying Man," which includes a quotation from Bach's aria "Es ist vollbracht," from the *St. John Passion*, BWV 245.

22. This is another instance in which Worrell received no official (i.e., remunerative) credit for his work. Credit is given only to Ruth Copeland and Phil Trim. It is not even clear from the album information that this song is a cover. Clinton himself seems not to have been aware of its origin;

the informed decision to use harpsichord, a keyboard instrument appropriate to the baroque era but seldom encountered in funk. Worrell's choices here clearly reveal not only historical knowledge but also a multifaceted progressive vision expressed through his musical ecumenicism.

Multiple, separate, identifiable musical styles emerge from Worrell's keyboard commentary on arguably every P-Funk track. They were certainly informed by the repertory he studied at the conservatory but also beyond. In one of the band's signature songs, "P-Funk (Wants to Get Funked Up)," Worrell references at least three different styles in extremely close proximity: funk, "classical," and blues.[23] The greatest kaleidoscopic mixture of musics occurs toward the end of the track (approximately seven minutes in), where Worrell participates in the funk groove, adds fistfuls of virtuosic chords right out of the concert hall repertory, and then switches to a blues piano texture, all within the space of less than a minute. What triggered his musical imagination to go in these directions is probably unknowable. Whatever the explanation, Worrell's characteristic mixture works and represents in microcosm the eclectic blend that is specifically P-Funk. Even Broadway musicals make their appearance. For example, Worrell injects a direct, though brief, quotation from Gershwin's "I Got Rhythm" into "Give Up the Funk (Tear the Roof Off the Sucker)" (2:43–2:44).[24] Worrell answers the vocalists' refrain, "there's a whole lotta rhythm going round," purely instrumentally with Gershwin's melodic tag to the words, "Who could ask for anything more?" The topical connection between foreground and background is, in this case, obvious.

The creative impulse behind Worrell's concert-hall stylings in "Aquaboogie" are much more difficult to pin down.[25] His additions in this case owe everything to the classical tradition.[26] The liquid subject of "Aquaboogie" might explain the journey of Worrell's improvisatory imagination. After all, there is piano repertory associated with underwater topics (such as Ravel's *Ondine* or Debussy's *Sunken Cathedral*). Perhaps it was works like these that inspired his decision to add to the already busy texture big,

---

he gives all credit for the music and text to Ruth Copeland (Clinton, *Brothas Be*, 88). Judging from Worrell's original manuscripts, the musical arrangement of the Pop Tops' song for Parliament's use was entirely his. I thank Mrs. Worrell for sending digital images of these materials (Judie Worrell, e-mail message to author, 5 June 2019).

23. Parliament, *Mothership Connection*, Casablanca NBLP 7022, 1975, 33⅓ rpm.

24. Ibid.

25. Parliament, *Motor Booty Affair*, Casablanca NBLP 7125, 1978, 33⅓ rpm.

26. In his memoir, Clinton claims that the bass line in "Aquaboogie" was "something Bernie translated from a classical cello part" (*Brothas Be*, 204). I have not been able to verify this detail. It has also been said that the keyboard bass line in this instance was not Worrell's but Walter "Junie" Morrison's. Both men are no longer with us, so the question remains open.

romantic, planed chords (from about 4:30 to the end of the track). For reasons utterly unexplainable, the tune "Mary Had a Little Lamb" also makes its appearance (6:18). Considering the abject lunacy that is the rest of this gloriously postmodern track, also referred to as "(A Psychoalphadiscobetabioaquadoloop)," effectively nothing could be out of place. Why not insert a passage of virtuosic chords? They certainly help depict the uncertain depths of aquatic spaces through their wide range and floating, nonfunctional harmonies. These aspects of "Aquaboogie" might be understood as another manifestation of what Clinton recognized as Worrell's love for "Bach." Worrell spent years perfecting this material at the conservatory, and it all came together to produce a richly communicative, multifaced musical language that no other funk band could offer.

The most Bachian track in the P-Funk/Funkadelic catalog is not "Aquaboogie" or Clinton's putative "Nappy Dugout," though, but is instead "Atmosphere," from the 1975 album *Let's Take It to the Stage*.[27] As such, it warrants closer attention. In "Oh Lord, Why Lord," we have an example of Worrell playing variations over a baroque canon; in his solo keyboard accompaniment for "Atmosphere," he again draws on his formal training in historical styles to create an improvised fugue unmistakably in the manner of J. S. Bach (see Example 5.1). The result is an extraordinary, seven-minute, contrapuntally inspired keyboard tour de force paired, for some reason, with a short scrap of crude poetry recited by George Clinton.[28] The sophistication and extent of Worrell's music provides stark contrast to Clinton's sixty seconds of senseless obscenity. Clinton delivers his text with mock formality ("Good evening, boys and girls . . ."), which renders its actual contents—all of which are most definitely inappropriate for children—all the

27. Funkadelic, *Let's Take It to the Stage*, Westbound W-215, 1975, 33⅓ rpm.

28. The text to Clinton's poem is as follows:

> Good evening, boys and girls
> Welcome to another evening of
> "I hate that word called dick"
> It goes like this:
>
> I hate that word called "dick"
> It sounds so awfully thick
> So I think I'll call it "prick"
> 'Cause I hate that word called "dick"
>
> Ha ha ha ha!
>
> I hate that word called "pussy"
> It sounds so awfully squishy
> So I guess I'll call it "clit"
> 'Cause I hate that word called "pussy"

Example 5.1. "Atmosphere," fugal exposition (mm. 1–35).
(Transcribed by Shaoai Ashley Zhang and Andrew Steinberg.)

Example 5.1. Continued.

more jarring. The ironic clash in this track between the learned and the lewd seems, in fact, to be its sole reason for being. Clinton's three stanzas of locker-room profanity are entirely devoid of poetic value: from a technical standpoint, they only casually engage with the protocols of regular meter and rhyme; from a rhetorical standpoint, they are hopeless. This song's purpose can only be to shock, which is sometimes an expressive end in itself and one that is certainly integral to P-Funk's overall aesthetic.

Given the content of Clinton's text, Worrell's musical invocation of Bach in this particular instance is puzzling. Why an explicitly Bachian style for this song and literally no other? What in Clinton's poem could possibly have inspired this musical response? Due to Worrell's passing, these questions may never be put to rest. What we do know about P-Funk's usual recording process, though, is that tone and text were generally created separately, as Clinton reported with regard to "Nappy Dugout" ("my job was to make my point and get out of the way. The final step was to let Bernie take his shot at it, add his keyboard parts around the bass").[29] Judie Worrell, Bernie's wife, has also been clear on P-Funk's segmented compositional process, but according to her recollection, the order of operations was exactly the opposite of what Clinton describes. She reports that Bernie's music came first, not last, and the final step was actually Clinton's addition of text: "Many times, (in fact I think all the time), Bernie would lay down tracks and then George would come in later and put down his obscenity-laced insanity. Bernie NEVER played to the words. NEVER. Not once. A good example of that is 'Flashlight.' Bernie did the tracks and brought them to George and then George mumbled his crazy over it."[30] Given the conflicting firsthand witness accounts, one can only wonder whether the process was the same every time. There is in fact reason to suspect that the routine was malleable according to the demands of the situation. For example, Mrs. Worrell gives the example of "Flashlight," where Bernie's musical contribution certainly came first. As a counterexample, Bernie's improvised, Gershwin-inspired commentary on "Give Up the Funk (Tear the Roof Off the Sucker)" can only have been created in response to the lyrics. Thus, there might have been a general working pattern, but there is also evidence of artistic exchange. It should also be borne in mind that the case of "Atmosphere" might have been somewhat exceptional because it involved only two musicians—Worrell and Clinton—rather than the entire band. The standard operating procedure, whatever it might have been, might not have applied.

We cannot unequivocally determine whether the text or the music came first in the case of "Atmosphere," but either Clinton was reacting to Worrell's fugue or Worrell was

29. Clinton, *Brothas Be*, 118.

30. Judie Worrell, e-mail message to author, 8 August 2019.

reacting to Clinton's poem. Either way, the conclusion is the same: deliberate contrast must have been the goal. If Clinton was intentionally reacting with undisciplined filth to what he perceived as a learned style in Worrell's improvisation, the choice would align with Clinton's general modus operandi, which was always to provoke. If Worrell chose a learned style to accompany Clinton's lyrics, then perhaps the idea was antidote. In life, Worrell was neither habitually vulgar nor aggressively provocative. It would have been a stroke of genius for him to have crafted for this text a musical setting so sophisticated that its quality alone highlighted the true baseness of Clinton's contribution. No matter which came first (although one suspects it was the music), Worrell's fugal improvisation betrays his acute musical intelligence, at once unmistakably skilled and darkly, amusingly cartoonish. This track continues to have value solely because of Worrell's captivating accompaniment. Clinton's text is mostly in the way.

For the dazzling brilliance it contains, "Atmosphere" ranks fourth among *Rolling Stone*'s "10 Essential Tracks from the P-Funk Keyboardist," where it is colorfully described as

> a bewildering blur of the comic and the deathly. . . . Shifting from the Hammond B-3 to a Minimoog synth, Worrell breathes aching, absurd pathos into technology's alien oscillations, skulking like a calliope player in a haunted amusement park . . ., *sucking the blood of a Bach fugue like an Afro-futurist fiend*, and presiding over a hushed church service . . ., before flipping it all into proggy laserium melancholy. It was later sampled by Prince Paul for his dazzling DJ turn on Stetsasonic's "Music for the Stetfully Insane," in addition to providing the primal ooze from which horrorcore rap emerged (see Gravediggaz and Three 6 Mafia).[31] (emphasis mine)

There are several useful pieces of information in this quotation, among them that Worrell's music for "Atmosphere" in particular inspired the creation of yet more music ("Music for the Stetfully Insane" as well as the entire genre of horrorcore rap), which is the definition of influence in popular music. These new works therefore carry not only Worrell's musical DNA into the future but, through him, Bach's as well.

Rolling Stone's authors are not the only ones to equate Worrell's musical style in "Atmosphere" with Bach's. The artistic debt was also noted by way of remembrance in a *Hollywood Reporter* article immediately following Worrell's death: "On Funkadelic's 'Atmosphere,' his chatty organ prelude, like a mash-up of Bach and 'The Munsters

---

31. Charles Aaron and Mosi Reeves, "Bernie Worrell: 10 Essential Tracks from the P-Funk Keyboardist," *Rolling Stone*, 24 June 2016, accessed 14 March 2019, https://www.rollingstone.com/music/music-lists/bernie-worrell-10-essential-tracks-from-the-p-funk-keyboardist-25062/funkadelic-free-your-mind-and-your-ass-will-follow-1970-162689/.

Theme,' set up some of Clinton's more unprintable lyrics."[32] It is perhaps obvious but still worth pointing out that in both of these articles, the journalists felt safe in relying on popular recognition of one particular corner of Bach's art: his organ preludes and fugues. One suspects that the cultural work of Disney's 1940 film *Fantasia*, with its illustration of the embattled Toccata and Fugue in D Minor, BWV 565, is at least partly to thank.

The potency of the popular image of Bach the contrapuntist makes sense because effective references to his vocal works or secular instrumental music would require a receiving audience with extensive, highly specialized, "classical" training. Furthermore, any such references would likely have to be direct quotations rather than imitations "in the style of": imitation is what we have in the example of "Atmosphere." There is a certain irony here in that Bach, in his earliest reception history, was mostly known as a composer of contrapuntal keyboard works. Nearly three hundred years later, and in spite of all that we have learned about him since, this association still dominates. One significant difference between Bach's reception in the eighteenth century and the twenty-first, though, is that his learned, contrapuntal style was originally perceived as an artistic failing, or poor marketing acumen (ask Johann Adolph Scheibe). It has since been transformed into a symbol of ultimate musical accomplishment, and the name "Bach" has come to signify the pinnacle of "high art" concert-culture in the Western musical tradition.

Generic use of Bach's name to signal formal musical training (rather than the specific use to indicate detailed compositional kinship) also occurs in discussions of Worrell's art. In yet another *Rolling Stone* article, the critic Mark Binelli links the two composers and mentions counterpoint but does not anchor his observations with reference to any track in particular: "From the beginning, P-Funk had included [Eddie] Hazel and Bernie Worrell, a classically trained pianist whose wild, contrapuntal keyboard melodies came straight out of Bach."[33] Binelli's characterization of Worrell's melodies might have been informed by what he heard in the band's discography and his knowledge of the keyboardist's background, but he might also have been reflexively responding to what Clinton (or his collaborating writer) said about "Nappy Dugout." Perhaps he simply parroted uncritically the statement that Worrell had used Bach's theory of counterpoint to generate his music.

---

32. Associated Press, "Bernie Worrell, Parliament Funkadelic Keyboardist, Dies at 72," *Hollywood Reporter*, 24 June 2016, accessed 14 March 2019, https://www.hollywoodreporter.com/news/bernie -worrell-dead-parliament-funkadelic-906286.

33. Mark Binelli, "George Clinton: Doctor Atomic," *Rolling Stone*, 27 April 2015, accessed 17 April 2017, http://www.rollingstone.com/music/features/george-clinton-doctor-atomic-20150427.

Clinton's remarkably precise mention of counterpoint in the case of "Nappy Dugout" is puzzling, raising the question of what it was about that song that caused him to invoke the name of Bach in the first place. One possibility is that he confused "Nappy Dugout" for "Atmosphere" because they share a common topic.[34] Another possibility is that, in this instance, Clinton is also using Bach's name in its generic sense without a clear understanding of what he is actually implying from a compositional standpoint. As we have seen, not all of Worrell's melodies "came straight out of Bach," and certainly not the music in "Nappy Dugout." Clinton's invocation of Bach and counterpoint, like Binelli's after him, are probably best understood as examples of the generic use of Bach's name as an all-encompassing stand-in for musical practices related to formal training in traditionally European concert-hall genres.[35]

As we know, Worrell's background included a lot of formal training. His contribution to the band is where seemingly disparate musical worlds came together to produce something entirely original and new: the P-Funk. Once again, in the words of funk scholar Rickey Vincent: "In perhaps the most powerfully symbolic union of the Funk Era, Worrell's competence in classical European musical forms collided and combined with the band's twisted black urban sensibilities to generate a bizarre dichotomy of perspectives—as if Shakespeare and Stagger Lee were dropping acid together in da hood."[36] Clinton wrote that Worrell "liked Bach quite a bit," and while Worrell's biography unfortunately does not bear out a specific affection for Bach in any detail (Mozart is the winner), it does amply support the idea that he "liked Bach" in the more generic sense of Bach as representative of "classical" music and the principles of formal composition.

Worrell's enviably innate musicality was such that he was able to move freely among musical styles and was particularly well versed in concert-hall keyboard literature, as can be inferred from the fact of his study at the New England Conservatory. Echoes of the concert pianist's training resound throughout P-Funk's discography, as we have seen. Archival documents from NEC allow a detailed view into the repertory Worrell studied and offer a clear explanation for the extraordinary technical and stylistic range

34. Slips of memory would also not be out of the question. Clinton's long-term use of psychedelic drugs and a significant crack habit surely had a cognitive impact. About it, he once commented, "Before, I thought if it wasn't for flashbacks I didn't have any memory, but once I got started, it [the book] started unraveling in pretty good sequence." See Andrew Purcell, "Parliament's George Clinton Untangles His Funkadelic Life and Gets Straight Down to Business," *Sydney Morning Herald*, 26 December 2014, accessed 22 March 2019, https://www.smh.com.au/entertainment/parliaments-george-clinton -untangles-his-funkadelic-life-and-gets-straight-down-to-business-20141219-12arai.html.

35. The names Beethoven and Mozart also exist in the popular imagination but connote different aspects of music-making: Mozart is the child prodigy; Beethoven, the mad, emotive genius. For better and worse, Bach seems to represent establishment discipline.

36. Vincent, *Funk*, 235.

he displayed at the P-Funk keyboards.[37] We see from the documents that Bach's works were part of Worrell's repertory from the beginning and were in fact among those that he performed at his entrance audition on June 30, 1962:[38]

1. Bach, Prelude and Fugue No. 8 [*WTC* I or II?]
2. Bach, Organ Prelude [unspecified]
3. Chopin, Etude Op. 10, No. 5
4. Tcherepnin, Bagatelles
5. Beethoven, Sonata Op. 53 ("Waldstein")

His improvised counterpoint in "Atmosphere" thirteen years later would seem to owe little to whichever "Prelude and Fugue No. 8" he performed in those early years, and without more information regarding which of Bach's organ preludes he studied, we can come to no detailed conclusions about its possible impact on his compositional future. Exact quotation is hardly the point, though, because it is Worrell's unmistakable and convincing reference to Bach's contrapuntal style in general that characterizes his music for "Atmosphere."

Worrell's annual performance evaluation sheets ("promotional" or "jury" sheets) are another source of information about his conservatory experiences and repertory. He obviously continued to study Bach's music alongside major works of the Romantic piano canon as the years unfolded. In June 1963, for example, he performed for the piano faculty pieces by Bach (unspecified) and Ravel (also unspecified). The reviews were mixed, and the faculty comments were a poor indication of his future success. Criticisms of his execution of Bach's music included these:[39]

1. Failed to understand problems of style
2. Starts phrases too loud
3. Rhythm in Bach!!!!!!! [with seven exclamation points]
4. Rather pale and uninteresting

One wonders whether the problem here was Worrell or the piano jury's concept in the early 1960s of what Bach should sound like. "Pale and uninteresting" and lacking in "rhythm" were certainly not predictors of Worrell's eventual musical voice.

---

37. Following admission to the conservatory, Worrell's recital programs included works such as Beethoven's Trio in E-flat Major, op. 1, no. 1 (US-Bc, Recital Program, New England Conservatory of Music, 13 January 1966), as well as two Schubert impromptus (op. 90, nos. 2 and 3) (US-Bc, Recital Program, New England Conservatory of Music, 19 December 1963).

38. Worrell, Admissions Application ("Audition Program"), 30 June 1962, New England Conservatory of Music, Student Record (registrar's office).

39. Worrell, Promotional Sheets, June 1963, New England Conservatory of Music, Student Record (registrar's office).

These promotional sheets are witnesses not only to the repertory Worrell learned and the progress that he made but also to the cultural resistance he encountered as a young black man studying classical music in 1960s Boston. A couple of the promotional sheets from his file do, in fact, contain evidence of racist language. For example, some of the professors consistently refer to him, but not to other male students, as "boy"; others describe him as "lazy." One of the professors does both. These might have been careless comments, made without particular intent, but because "boy" and "lazy" were also terms then applied pejoratively specifically to African Americans, suspicion rises. By way of contrast, other jury sheets refer to Worrell as "young man" or "student" and do not characterize him as lazy. Thus, the repetitions of "boy" and "lazy" in a couple of the sheets stand out all the more.

A survey of the other thirteen surviving sets of piano promotional sheets from the years in which Worrell was a student reveal, in fact, that no other male student was referred to repeatedly as "boy" and that those white students whose technical problems were surely related to lack of effort were not called "lazy." In place of dismissive criticism, they were instead prescribed personalized programs of study to address their deficiencies.[40] It is similarly disappointing in this context that Worrell's private piano teacher thought it necessary to convey his racial identity to the NEC admissions committee.[41] The act is especially conspicuous because this information was not included in her official letter of recommendation, even though there was ample room left for it on the page. Instead, Worrell's teacher sent this detail separately on a page of private stationery.[42] Worrell's wife, Judie, also reports that when Worrell would show up to his lessons at NEC, his studio teacher (Miklos Schwalb) would often close the music book and ask Bernie to "play some jazz" instead.[43] The teacher seems to have assumed that because Worrell was black, he wanted to play jazz. Worrell's talent was such that he could indeed play in any style, but jazz was never his focus, and it was not what he

40. Faculty referred to the eight other male students in the promotional sheets as: "Mr. [X]," "Student," "He," and "lad." The only other time the word "boy" was applied was to an Iranian student (File 16). Among the five female students, one faculty member only refers to them consistently by gender ("talented girl"; "musical girl"). No other student is referred to as lazy. One was said to be "dynamically weak" and "somewhat pallid" and chose repertory that was too easy (File 4), yet no one described him as lazy.

41. Worrell's teacher was Fay Barnaby Kent, herself once a student of the legendary Edward MacDowell. She was among those who worked to endow the MacDowell artists' colony in Peterborough, N.H. Her educational legacy would be another interesting avenue of research.

42. Barnaby Kent wrote, "Bernard is of the negro race." She also went on to explain how gifted Worrell was and how sad she was to lose him as a student.

43. Mrs. Worrell's recollection is corroborated by Bernie in Rogers, "Bernie Worrell Was the Key": "When I'd get to my teacher's for my weekly lesson, half the lesson, he'd say, 'Play some jazz.' So I'd improvise and [Schwalb] was hooked."

had entered NEC in order to study. In fact, his training prior to entering conservatory was entirely Eurocentric:

> I started out playing Schubert Impromptus, a little Bach, Beethoven Sonatas, and a lot of Mozart—I liked him, but I can never remember the opus numbers. And of course there were the Hanon studies. Classical music was all I played. I knew church music, because I'd played for Baptist church teas and backed my mother up when she sang at funerals, but I had no idea what R&B or rock and roll were; I heard bits and pieces over the radio, but I was never allowed to listen to too much of it. I didn't even know who Elvis Presley was![44]

Worrell would have preferred that his studio lessons at the conservatory be spent learning from his teacher rather than entertaining him. It is some comfort that in a later interview he stated that no one at the conservatory "messed with him" on the basis of his race. Whatever was going on behind the scenes seems therefore to have been reasonably well contained, at least from Worrell's student perspective, although it was clearly a background factor for some.[45]

Even though Worrell's formal musical education was fundamentally classical, we learn from later interviews that his informal musical experience before (but especially after) arriving at NEC was in fact quite varied and ultimately defining. Once in Boston, he expanded his horizons, and they stretched to include many different repertories, fluency in which ended up being vital to his future career:

> [Worrell's] move to Boston still had a decisive effect on his music, because it allowed him to follow his own interests more freely, without the immediate conservative influence of his family. "I went wild," he states. "Everything I'd kept inside just busted out. I stayed away from school and started hanging out. Boston was where I started playing in clubs. I got myself a job with the house band at Basin Street. You know Jim Nash, the football player with the New England Patriots? That was his club, and I backed up a lot of people there, like the Tavares, who were Chubby And The Turnpikes back then—I was with them for about two years—and [singers] Tammi Terrell, Freddie Scott, and Valerie Holiday, who is with the Three Degrees now. She didn't have any vocal training, so I helped her out and coached her. She also won the Miss Tan Boston contest; they called it 'Tan' back then," he adds with a laugh.[46]

In a 2011 interview with Alex del Zoppo at the ASCAP Expo, Worrell explained that in addition to his Boston nightclub work, he was also well versed in the musical

44. Bob Doerschuk, "Bernie Worrell, P-Funk's Multi-Keyboard Whiz," *Keyboard Magazine*, 19 July 2016, updated 29 November 2017, accessed 21 March 2019, https://www.keyboardmag.com/artists/bernie-worrell-p-funks-multi-keyboard-whiz. Reprint of an interview from the 1978 issue of *Contemporary Keyboard*.

45. Rogers, "Bernie Worrell Was the Key."

46. Doerschuk, "Bernie Worrell, P-Funk's Multi-Keyboard Whiz."

traditions of different religions. When del Zoppo suggested that Worrell must be glad that he had "given up the classical stuff" to play instead with P-Funk, Worrell corrected him, explaining that this was not the case at all:

AdZ: Aren't you glad you did that then and kinda gave up the classical stuff?

BW: Well, I didn't exactly give it up. What I do, for people that really know, I mix musics together.

AdZ: Ah.

BW: So I think that's what made P-Funk a little different than your other funk genres. Because I would always intertwine the classical feel with the funk or Latin. It's one of the gifts—another of the gifts I had. Interject some cartoon music into it. So it's another gift. I was able to mix musics.

I was raised Catholic, came up in the Baptist church also. I was an organist for the Episcopal Church. Played accompaniments for a Jewish men's chorus while I was in college in Boston. So all those influences, I just take it in when I'm creating or writing.[47]

Worrell's non-conservatory musical experiences were clearly as important to his future as his classical training, arguably even more so. Although certain conservatory faculty judged him "lazy" on his promotional sheets, Worrell was clearly anything but. It might have been the case, though, that his extracurricular musical activities resulted in fewer hours dedicated to practicing the classics. In the long run, Worrell ended up a far more versatile and well-rounded musician for it.

One of Worrell's last collaborators, the Scottish funk musician Jesse Rae, had these words to say about how Worrell's classical training merged with his career as a popular musician:

The structure o' Classical Music, obviously was educational, and meant that he could write all the Charts for everyone, Strings and horns, but because his genius was God given, he had the ability tae "think oot o' the Box" and would often get annoyed when Classical was put on a pedestal o' snobbery. He felt who ever the composer . . . they would want it tae be accessible tae all. No boundaries between different types o' Music frae a' around the World. He often referred tae how funky Mozart was.[48]

There is, of course, no direct mention of Bach here (only Mozart), but the message of blended musical styles is consistent with what Worrell said of his own art and intentions. According to Rae, Worrell is the inventor of "Classical Funk," a category unto itself, whose chief distinguishing characteristic is permeable stylistic boundaries.

---

47. "An Interview with Bernie Worrell, Legendary Musician, with Alex del Zoppo," YouTube video, 13:00, 16 June 2011, accessed 21 March 2019, https://youtu.be/ztSMeB-Gmug. This portion of the interview occurs at 5:45.

48. Jesse Rae, e-mail message to author, 20 April 2018.

Worrell's extracurricular musical exploration during his college years also included another transformative influence: exposure to the English prog-rock band Emerson, Lake and Palmer. Keith Emerson was among the very first rock musicians to use Moog synthesizers, and Worrell clearly found the musical possibilities irresistible: "I wasn't really interested in technology, but when I was in college, at the New England Conservatory in Boston, I used to listen to Emerson, Lake & Palmer. I loved the *Tarkus* album. Keith was the first guy I heard using the Moog. I liked the sound of that album and the things he was doing with the instrument."[49] Worrell's own ingenious use of Robert A. Moog's keyboard technology would shape the rest of his performing life and was another element that would distinguish him among popular musicians and, by extension, the bands with whom he played, especially P-Funk.

Not insignificant in this context is that the first musician Keith Emerson heard use the Moog was none other than Wendy Carlos, on her 1968 album *Switched-On Bach*.[50] There is no evidence that Worrell knew this album, but his use of a Moog on "Atmosphere" to render a Bachian fugue certainly has undeniable similarities with Carlos's radical undertaking. Because *Switched-On Bach* won three Grammy Awards, it would be somewhat surprising if Worrell had not somehow encountered it. Along with Carlos and Emerson, Worrell is now widely acknowledged as one of the most influential early adopters of Moog's technology.[51] His timbral and compositional choices on "Atmosphere" link it with Carlos's contemporary work, whether or not the similarities were intentional.

The impact of Worrell's Moog-enabled soundscape on popular music genres today can hardly be exaggerated. We have become so used to the presence of electronic instruments that it is easy to forget that the practice began somewhere. According to Rickey Vincent, the electronic component of P-Funk is among its most pivotal contributions: "Among their fundamental ingredients that still reign in black pop today are the electronic 'clap' sound, a synthesizer-bass (a bass track played on a keyboard), a shrewdly displayed image of political (and sexual) awareness, and a penchant for elaborately layered horn and vocal lines, often creating a synthesis of European chord

49. Joe Bosso, "Bernie Worrell Talks Vintage Synths, ELP, Parliament/Funkadelic, Talking Heads and More," *musicradar*, 11 June 2013, accessed 21 March 2019, https://www.musicradar.com/news/tech/bernie-worrell-talks-vintage-synths-elp-parliament-funkadelic-talking-heads-and-more-576154?fbclid=IwAR3bdhNpbcYhKk8ToQBa9dEnUSbb19b4JNd7XEoCkqPZufwO1f_erlsIQ7g.

50. "Like many others, Emerson first discovered the Moog in 1968, when he heard Walter (later Wendy) Carlos's *Switched-On Bach*." See "Is a Moog Renaissance Nigh?," *Wired*, 20 May 2004, accessed 14 March 2019, https://www.wired.com/2004/05/is-a-moog-renaissance-nigh/.

51. There are numerous references to Worrell's early and influential use of Moog's keyboards. Moog's own website is only one among them: https://www.moogmusic.com/news/wizard-family-lasting-legacy-bernie-worrell.

structure and African rhythm grooves into a large, ensemble sound."[52] Importantly, the musical innovations Vincent lists were nearly all Worrell's legacy to P-Funk, from the use of electronic media to the clap tracks, the layered horn and vocal lines, and most certainly the European chord structure.

That Bach's musical style informs even a small part of the extraordinary product that is P-Funk reveals the extent to which his music has become a widely recognized symbol. In one sense, it is so celebrated that it transcends boundaries and is said to be universal in that it belongs to everyone. Paradoxically, though, its inclusion in popular repertories (and arguably in any sphere outside of its culture of origin) also trades in its power to signify a musical and cultural Other, which can sometimes be understood as a symbol of privilege and access. That aspect of Bach's broader reception informs the generic meaning of "Bach" that Clinton invoked in stating that Worrell "liked Bach quite a bit." It was certainly not Bach in particular to whom he was referring but to Worrell's exclusive training, even though Bach's style did actually play a role both directly and indirectly in P-Funk's music, as we have seen.

Worrell's inclusion of Bach's style in P-Funk served the band's stated mission, which was never to divide but to unite and to empower, to be "a celebration of the earthy, funky, emotionally vital way of life; a cosmology of 'oneness' in which everything and everyone in the universe is interconnected."[53] Worrell was the musical embodiment of that cosmology. He achieved extraordinary stylistic synthesis because he was a musician's musician: he could play the most complex notated literature as well as improvise in every style he heard. His virtuosic fluency is what enabled the band to speak in many tongues, to musically represent P-Funk's vital notion of The One. In reflecting on the path he had taken in getting there, Worrell dismissed the concept of generic boundaries:

> "Your technique does go down over the years from playing rock," he admits, "and my mother is kind of disappointed that I didn't become a classical musician. I'm glad that I had that kind of training; I think everyone who plays keyboards should go through it, although not everybody is going to. I liked classical music, but I couldn't go for how they would talk about rock and roll or R&B back then. They put classical music up on a pedestal. Well, the hell with that! Music is music, and that's what it all boils down to."[54]

Fundamentally, Worrell believed that no style was superior to another, just as no human being was superior to another. In this band, and especially in Worrell, musical worlds united to become one, and there is a little something for—and of—everyone, including J. S. Bach.

52. Vincent, *Funk*, 231.

53. Ibid., 258.

54. Doerschuk, "Bernie Worrell, P-Funk's Multi-Keyboard Whiz."

CONTRIBUTORS

LAURA BUCH is an editor of *C. P. E. Bach: The Complete Works*, a project of The Packard Humanities Institute in Cambridge, Massachusetts.

STEPHEN A. CRIST is professor of music history at Emory University.

ELLEN EXNER is a full-time member of the New England Conservatory's music history and musicology faculty.

MOIRA LEANNE HILL is a musicologist who resides in Northfield, Minnesota.

ERINN E. KNYT is associate professor of music history at the University of Massachusetts Amherst.

MARKUS ZEPF, musicologist and organist, is a research fellow at the Bach-Archiv, Leipzig.

GENERAL INDEX

INDEX OF WORKS

Bach Perspectives
is a publication of the
American Bach Society,
dedicated to promoting the study
and performance of the music of
Johann Sebastian Bach.
Membership information is available online at
www.americanbachsociety.org.

THE BACH PERSPECTIVES SERIES

The University of Illinois Press
is a founding member of the
Association of American University Presses.

Composed in 10/14 Janson Text
by Jim Proefrock
at the University of Illinois Press
Manufactured by Sheridan Books, Inc.

University of Illinois Press
1325 South Oak Street
Champaign, IL 61820-6903
www.press.uillinois.edu